BARBECUE COOKBOOK

Carol Bowen

Hamlyn

London New York Sydney Toronto

Acknowledgements

Front cover photograph by John Lee
Photographs on pages 55, 65, 68, 77, 78, 96, 113, 114
by Christian Délu/PAF International.
Photograph on page 38 by John Lee, courtesy of Tower
Housewares Limited. All other photography by Vic Paris
of Alphaplus Studios, Leatherhead.
Line drawings by Ann Rees and Tony Streek

Published by Hamlyn Publishing,
a division of The Hamlyn Publishing Group Ltd,
Bridge House, London Road, Twickenham, Middlesex,
England

ISBN 0 600 32649 7

Phototypeset by Servis Filmsetting Ltd, Manchester
Printed in Yugoslavia

CONTENTS

USEFUL FACTS AND FIGURES

Notes on metrication

In this book quantities are given in metric and Imperial measures. Exact conversion from Imperial to metric measures does not usually give very convenient working quantities and so the metric measures have been rounded off into units of 25 grams. The table below shows the recommended equivalents.

Ounces	Approx g to nearest whole figure	Recom- mended conversion to nearest unit of 25	Ounces	Approx g to nearest whole figure	Recom- mended conversion to nearest unit of 25
1	28	25	11	312	300
2	57	50	12	340	350
3	85	75	13	368	375
4	113	100	14	396	400
5	142	150	15	425	425
6	170	175	16 (1 lb)	454	450
7	198	200	17	482	475
8	227	225	18	510	500
9	255	250	19	539	550
10	283	275	20 (1¼ lb)	567	575

Note When converting quantities over 20 oz first add the appropriate figures in the centre column, then adjust to the nearest unit of 25. As a general guide, 1 kg (1000 g) equals 2.2 lb or about 2 lb 3 oz. This method of conversion gives good results in nearly all cases, although in certain pastry and cake recipes a more accurate conversion is necessary to produce a balanced recipe.

Liquid measures The millilitre has been used in this book and the following table gives a few examples.

Imperial	Approx ml to nearest whole figure	Recom- mended ml	Imperial	Approx ml to nearest whole figure	Recom- mended ml
¼ pint	142	150 ml	1 pint	567	600 ml
½ pint	283	300 ml	1½ pints	851	900 ml
¾ pint	425	450 ml	1¾ pints	992	1000 ml (1 litre)

Spoon measures All spoon measures given in this book are level unless otherwise stated.

Can sizes At present, cans are marked with the exact (usually to the nearest whole number) metric equivalent of the Imperial weight of the contents, so we have followed this practice when giving can sizes.

Flour Either plain or self-raising flour can be used in the recipes unless specified.

Herbs Use fresh unless specified otherwise.

Oven temperatures

The table below gives recommended equivalents.

	°C	°F	Gas Mark		°C	°F	Gas Mark
Very cool	110	225	$\frac{1}{4}$	Moderately hot	190	375	5
	120	250	$\frac{1}{2}$		200	400	6
Cool	140	275	1	Hot	220	425	7
	150	300	2		230	450	8
Moderate	160	325	3	Very hot	240	475	9
	180	350	4				

Notes for American and Australian users

In America the 8-oz measuring cup is used. In Australia metric measures are now used in conjunction with the standard 250-ml measuring cup. The Imperial pint, used in Britain and Australia, is 20 fl oz, while the American pint is 16 fl oz. It is important to remember that the Australian tablespoon differs from both the British and American tablespoons; the table below give a comparison. The British standard tablespoon, which has been used throughout this book, holds 17.7 ml, the American 14.2 ml, and the Australian 20 ml. A teaspoon holds approximately 5 ml in all three countries.

British	American	Australian	British	American	Australian
1 teaspoon	1 teaspoon	1 teaspoon	$3\frac{1}{2}$ tablespoons	4 tablespoons	3 tablespoons
1 tablespoon	1 tablespoon	1 tablespoon	4 tablespoons	5 tablespoons	$3\frac{1}{2}$ tablespoons
2 tablespoons	3 tablespoons	2 tablespoons			

An Imperial/American guide to solid and liquid measures

Solid measures

IMPERIAL	AMERICAN
1 lb butter or margarine	2 cups
1 lb flour	4 cups
1 lb granulated or castor sugar	2 cups
1 lb icing sugar	3 cups
8 oz rice	1 cup

Liquid measures

IMPERIAL	AMERICAN
$\frac{1}{4}$ pint liquid	$\frac{2}{3}$ cup liquid
$\frac{1}{2}$ pint	$1\frac{1}{4}$ cups
$\frac{3}{4}$ pint	2 cups
1 pint	$2\frac{1}{2}$ cups
$1\frac{1}{2}$ pints	$3\frac{3}{4}$ cups
2 pints	5 cups ($2\frac{1}{2}$ pints)

Note When making any of the recipes in this book, only follow one set of measures as they are not interchangeable.

American terms

The list below gives some American equivalents or substitutes for terms and ingredients used in this book.

Equipment and terms

BRITISH/AMERICAN	BRITISH/AMERICAN
cling film/saran wrap	mince/grind
cocktail stick/toothpick	mould/mold
flan tin/pie pan	packet/package
foil/aluminum foil	piping bag/pastry bag
greaseproof paper/waxed paper	polythene/plastic
liquidise/blend	top and tail/stem and head

Ingredients

BRITISH/AMERICAN

aubergine/eggplant
bacon rasher/bacon slice
biscuit/cookie or cracker
black grapes/purple grapes
black olives/ripe olives
cauliflower sprigs/cauliflowerets
celery stick/celery stalk
chilli/chili pepper
cooking apple/baking apple
cornflour/cornstarch
courgettes/zucchini
demerara sugar/brown sugar
digestive biscuits/graham crackers
double cream/heavy cream
essence/extract
gelatine/gelatin

BRITISH/AMERICAN

green grapes/white grapes
ham/cured or smoked ham
hard-boiled eggs/hard-cooked eggs
lard/shortening
minced beef/ground beef
peeled prawn/shelled shrimp
root ginger/ginger root
seedless raisins/seeded raisins
single cream/light cream
soft brown sugar/light brown sugar
spring onion/scallion
stock cube/bouillon cube
sweetcorn/corn
tomato purée/tomato paste
unsalted butter/sweet butter
vanilla pod/vanilla bean

In spite of unpredictable weather, there is something irresistibly festive about eating out of doors. Perhaps it is the sight and aroma of food sizzling over a hot barbecue or the alfresco nature of cooking food out of doors instead of in a kitchen that makes the difference. A happy fact since no meal is more fun to prepare.

There is nothing very difficult about preparing meals in the open air, but a certain amount of basic knowledge helps to avoid some of the pitfalls, such as a smoky fire, food charred on the outside yet raw in the middle, and lukewarm drinks. It is hoped that this book will provide an easy guide to choosing and using the various types of barbecue available, managing the fire as well as preparing food for outdoor use. Help on the quantities of food to prepare are all important too, since fresh air sharpens appetites. There are ideas here for simple family meals through to grand parties.

Although relatively new in popularity in this country, millions of people all over the world enjoy the delights of barbecued food. I hope this book will give you all the advice you need to join them. Bon appétit!

Carol Bowen

ALL ABOUT BARBECUES

CHOOSING A BARBECUE

On a surprisingly warm spring day, sizzling summer afternoon or balmy, seemingly everlasting early autumn evening, the sound and aroma of food being cooked out of doors is unforgettable. Perhaps it is the tantalising flavour of charcoal-grilled food or the inevitable joy in discovering that everyone can join in with the cooking that makes barbecuing such a popular pastime. And, year by year, it is a pursuit that is becoming increasingly popular. Despite unpredictable weather more families and friends are gathering to enjoy the delights of barbecued food. In response, manufacturers are encouraging novices and devotees alike by supplying more efficient handy tools and equipment to make barbecuing less of a hit and miss affair and more of a pleasurable pastime.

Whether you have a large garden, postage-stamp patio or balcony, you too can join the barbecue enthusiasts, for the basics of barbecuing are really quite simple. All you need is cooking and serving equipment, fuel and food, a place to cook and a place to eat. However, within such a simple framework the choices are anything but easy.

The most expensive, and therefore the most important, item that you are likely to buy is the barbecue itself, so it pays to compare and consider the construction, capabilities, sturdiness, size, mobility, stability and ease of operation of many units before you opt for the one that most closely matches your needs – remembering of course that needs may change.

Choose a barbecue that is sturdy and stable laden as well as unladen; that will cope with regular cooking *and* entertaining needs or that is expansible, with additional folding grills to cope with larger than usual gatherings; that can be easily moved by wheels or handles if you intend to cook in more than one location; that can be left out of doors or stored easily during the winter months; and if a gas or electric barbecue is of the right size and construction, it will need to be located near to a fuel supply.

Barbecues, regardless of type, are manufactured in dozens of styles from the very simple to the stunningly sumptuous and sophisticated. In addition there are many kits available for building your own barbecue, again ranging from the basic to the specialist.

It is generally possible to recognise seven basic barbecue types. The hibachi, table-top portable, open brazier, covered or hooded kettle and wagon or barbecue box are all types of barbecue that are charcoal-fired; while kettle, wagon and single or double-unit barbecue box-shaped units and small open-grills or braziers are types that are also available as gas-fired or electrically heated units.

Hibachi

The hibachi is a small lightweight barbecue that is popular with beginners because of its low price and very simple operation. However, mobility is probably the hibachi's greatest virtue since it can be easily transferred from garage to garden, cupboard to balcony or car to beach and picnic table without fuss or bother.

Consisting of a heavy cast iron fire-bowl usually set upon wooden legs (removable in most cases), it has a single draught control at the front of the fire-bowl and multiple level grill positions.

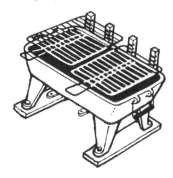

The smallest hibachi with a single grill area will cope with cooking for four hungry adults; if you intend to cook for more consider a double or triple hibachi or bank several single hibachis together.

Table-top Portable

As the name suggests these are small portable barbecues that are easily assembled and positioned on a table top for cooking. Usually consisting of a round 25–40-cm/10–16-inch diameter grill set on a metal fire-bowl supported by short telescopic, fold-up or screw-in legs, they will hold fuel to cook for about six adults at a time.

At the premium end of the market some table-top portable barbecues have a small wind shield, mini-rotisserie and adjustable grill.

Open Brazier

Once hooked on the delights of barbecue cooking most enthusiasts opt for a basic open brazier as their barbecue model. Needless to say it is within this group that most variety abounds – for you can choose from a simple no-fuss open brazier with easy controls to a sophisticated model complete with spit-roasting equipment, half-hood, wind shield, clip-on tray, condiment shelf and adjustable grill.

Most models stand on telescopic, fold-up, clip-on or screw-on legs and some have wheels for easy mobility. Check that they are sturdy and stable when in position. Invest in a model with a stainless steel fire-bowl if you intend it to last for a few years.

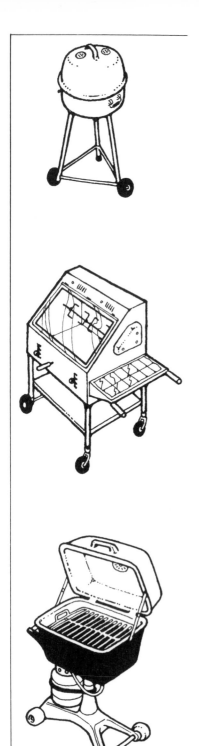

Covered or Hooded Kettle

A covered or hooded kettle barbecue is simply an open brazier model complete with hood. There, however, the similarity ends, for the hooded barbecue cooks food not only from below (via the charcoal) but also from above where heat is reflected back from the inside of the hood.

Controls are sophisticated on these models and devotees say they are as flexible as conventional indoor cookers. Temperature and speed of cooking are controlled mainly by dampers or vents which increase or decrease the draught, thereby speeding up or slowing down the heat from the fire-bowl. At the end of cooking the dampers are completely closed to snuff out the fire – an economical bonus if there is plenty of charcoal left.

Most models resemble a large kettle drum in size and shape, about 50 cm/20 inches in diameter, and will cook for 12 or more people. Usually set on three sturdy legs with wheels, they have all the sophisticated extras you would expect from a premium model and many come with good comprehensive instructions for smoking as well as barbecuing food.

Wagon or Barbecue Box

Wagon or barbecue box barbecues are very similar to hooded or kettle barbecues except that the fire-bowl is covered with a hinged rectangular or box cover instead of a hood, and is mounted on either a portable wagon or pedestal instead of legs.

Very much the Rolls Royce of barbecues, the wagon or barbecue box often has a temperature sensitive see-through oven box with built-in air temperature thermometer for accurate cooking, and many boast motorised spit or rotisserie baskets, smoking equipment, a multitude of handy oven attachments, convertible and adjustable grills, clip-on or built-in shelves and sometimes a special keep-warm second oven.

Gas and Electric Barbecues

Barbecues fuelled by liquefied petroleum gas or electricity are the answer if you want a traditional 'wood-fire or charcoal' flavour without the set-backs of using solid fuel or charcoal.

Barbecues that are heated and cook by electric coils come in a multitude of sizes, and gas barbecues that either use bottled gas or are fixed to a permanent gas supply likewise offer great variety.

All gas units and some electric models use ceramic lava rocks which rest on a grid above the burners or electric element and diffuse the heat evenly. Unlike charcoal, lava rock does not burn out and can be used time and time again. It still produces that delicious outdoor flavour you expect from a barbecue since it is the smoke from sizzling drippings, not the use of charcoal, that gives the barbecue flavour to foods.

A gas or an electric barbecue will not cook food any faster than the traditional barbecue but heating up times are generally shorter – about 10–15 minutes; there is no complicated fire-bed to prepare and no mess or ashes to clean up afterwards; the heat does tend to be of a more even and controllable nature; and cooling down is fast so safety standards are improved. Running costs can be lower than traditional barbecuing.

Site bottled gas barbecues on a stable surface and piped gas barbecues near to a gas outlet permanent line; position electric barbecues close to a suitable socket.

Barbecue buffs can choose from simple table-top models to grand wagon styles incorporating temperature controls, barbecue tools, self-cleaning operation, motorised rotisserie and push-button ignition (for gas).

Permanent Barbecues
With the ever-growing trend towards informal entertaining, many people have opted to make their barbecue a permanent outdoor feature. If you have the space and are quite willing to see it be used for a barbecue then a permanent barbecue area can be a splendid feature in a garden.

Choose a practical site that is sheltered but not too far from the house. If you don't have any natural vegetation cover then consider a canvas cover. Site so that any prevailing wind faces the open area of the barbecue – it will keep smoke away from the chef and help to encourage air into the fire-bed. As a minimum you will need a plot of flat ground about 60 × 120 cm/24 × 48 inches and at least a metre or good yard around for easy working.

The height of the grill area should ideally be waist high to prevent back-breaking cooking, and if space is no problem then consider adding on warming areas and shelves for cooking attachments, plates and food trays. You may already have a design in mind but if not you could build one from a specially designed kit. These generally consist of a charcoal grid, cooking grill,

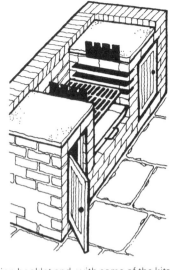

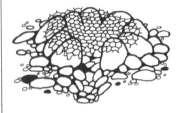

instruction booklet and, with some of the kits, battery-operated rotisserie – you simply have to buy the bricks and mortar yourself. Kits are quite expensive but they do result in attractive barbecues that blend beautifully into the garden setting.

For a much more economical version you could build one from a simple design published by the Brick Development Association. The beauty of this design is that it isn't strictly permanent and there are no storage problems. Using bricks but no mortar is a very effective solution for those who barbecue a great deal but do not want to have the restraints of a permanent barbecue. The leaflet is available free from the B.D.A., Woodside House, Winkfield, Windsor, Berkshire, if you enclose a s.a.e.

Impromptu barbecues

A multitude of items will easily convert or double-up as components of a simple if basic barbecue when the real thing is unavailable. For example, a punctured biscuit tin, old metal wheelbarrow, clay flowerpot or simple pebble base can all be used as a fire-bed base in the garden, in the country or on the beach, while chicken wire, an old oven-shelf or metal cooking rack could be used as the grid.

It is a great outdoor party idea to rig up a range of clay pot barbecues in which to cook a multitude of barbecue fare, from steaks to fruit snacks, with everyone lending a hand. Ideally use 23-cm/9-inch diameter deep clay flowerpots and line the inside of each with foil. Fill about one-third full with sand then top with a firelighter and about eight compressed charcoal briquettes. Stand the flowerpot on four bricks then light and leave to burn for 30 minutes. Top with chicken wire or a metal rack frame or place food across the top of the pot on long metal skewers to cook.

Fuel

Charcoal

Charcoal is by far and away the most popular form of barbecue fuel used today but wood is also popular.

Most charcoal available today is found in two forms – either as briquettes which are solid, pillow-like squares of compressed charcoal, or as lumpwood charcoal, irregular chunks of light wood-like charcoal. Charcoal briquettes have the edge over lumpwood charcoal when it comes to staying power but they are more expensive and generally more difficult to light (although some are impregnated with an ignition agent to make this easier). Charcoal is ideal fuel for the barbecue since it gives off little odour – it does, however, give off carbon monoxide so must *not* be used indoors.

For an average barbecue you will need about 30 briquettes of compressed charcoal for the fire-bed, or about nine briquettes for every 15-cm/6-inch square of fire-bed.

Wood

Wood makes a good barbecue fuel if you have a surplus. Soft woods such as pine, cedar and birch are good for kindling a fire since they burn quickly. Add harder woods later, such as oak, ash and beech, to burn more slowly and give a hotter fire.

THE FIRE

Where to set up the grill
Of prime importance when siting a barbecue is the aspect of safety – make sure yours is not positioned near to inflammable garden tubs, fencing or wooden structures, or near to burnable vegetation. Consider neighbours too so that they do not suffer the annoyance of fumes and smoke. Portable models can take advantage of their mobility by being positioned to best advantage on the particular day.

Building the fire
It is not essential but certainly effective to make a shallow bed of sand or gravel in the base of your barbecue upon which the charcoal or wood can sit. This helps to soak up excess fat drippings which can cause flare-ups and charring, and will protect the metal construction of the fire-bed. If cleanliness is one of the keynotes to your successful barbecuing then consider lining the fire-bed with foil, shiny side out, before adding the sand and charcoal – it makes clearing up afterwards very simple.

Lighting the fire
Everyone has their own favourite way to light the barbecue – choose from a fire chimney, liquid fire starter, firelighters, jellied alcohol, electric fire starters or a gas torch.

Fire chimneys
Specially devised fire chimneys are available for lighting the barbecue fire but it is easy to make one of your own. Simply remove the lid and bottom of a large cocoa tin or similar and punch holes just above the base all around the tin. Place the tin on the barbecue and stuff two wadded sheets of newspaper into the base. Stack the charcoal on top of the newspaper. Light the newspaper and leave the fire chimney to burn for 30 minutes by which time the charcoal is ready for use. Simply remove the chimney with gloves (to a secure place) and spread the coals to cook.

Liquid fire starters
Usually available in 1-litre plastic bottles, barbecue lighting fluid is a simple way to light a barbecue. Arrange the fire-bed of charcoal then spray liberally with the lighting fluid. Leave for about 2 minutes to soak in. Ignite the charcoal and leave to burn for 30-45 minutes until ready for use. Remember never to spray on to burning charcoal and to store away from naked flame or heat.

Firelighters
Firelighters are still perhaps the most popular, safe and sure way to ignite a charcoal or wood fire-bed without the fear of sparks, chemical residue and after-taste. Use about 3–4 blocks (measuring about 2·5 × 5 cm/1 × 2

inches) for an average fire-bed and simply light with a match. Coals ignited this way will be ready for cooking in 30–45 minutes.

Jellied alcohol
This is a highly combustible jelly-like fire starter for use in lighting barbecues and fires. Use about 1 tablespoon of jelly, dotted over the briquettes at the base of the fire-bed, for an average fire-bed. Light with a match – coals will be ready for cooking in about 30–45 minutes.

Electric fire starters
Resembling an electric element set on a long handle, this fire starter is placed in the fire-bed on a few coals. The remaining coals to be used are positioned on top of the starter. When plugged in and switched on the starter will ignite the briquettes in little under 10 minutes. The starter can then be removed or the heating element may burn out. The coals will be ready for cooking in a further 20–30 minutes.

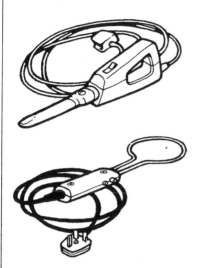

Gas torch
A gas torch or blow-lamp can be used to light a barbecue if liked. Aim the gas flame at the briquettes and hold in position until they catch a firm hold and visibly glow.

Building the fire-bed
A good fire-bed is not prepared by simply scattering a random pile of wood or charcoal. For best results, position wood and charcoal in a 'wig-wam' design. When ready the charcoal or wood can then be spread to make a solid flat bed ready for cooking. A solid flat fire-bed produces good even consistent heat for cooking most items, remembering that the closer the sticks or briquettes are to each other the hotter the fire-bed will be.

If you wish to cook by indirect heat where there is a good chance of flare-ups, especially with fatty meats, then build a divided bed of coals by banking a pile of coals either side of a metal drip pan.

To spit-roast with success build a fire-bed of solid coals to the back of the barbecue and place a metal drip pan under the rotating food in the centre of the grill area.

Barbecue rosemary chicken (see recipe page 59)

Managing the fire

A barbecue should be lit on average about 30–45 minutes before it is needed for cooking. You will know the fire is ready when the charcoal or wood is covered in a fine grey ash or it glows red by night. Sometimes when cooking for a large gathering you may need to add more coals or wood. Add these to the edge then move into the centre after they have started to burn – this way you do not reduce the temperature of the fire too quickly.

Cooking heat can be varied in a number of ways: adjust the distance between grid and fire-bed; increase or decrease the amount of fuel or space further apart the fuel you already have; and brush away the ash from the coals or use bellows to get a fiercer heat. For example, for a hotter fire and increased cooking speed use any one or all of the following techniques: position the grid nearer to the fire, increase the draught, push the coals nearer together, brush away any fine ash and use bellows if necessary.

Snuffing the fire

When you have finished cooking and if there is little fuel left then leave the barbecue to die down as you would an ordinary fire. Protect with a fireguard if young children are around. If the fire-bed still has some good usable charcoal on board then remove with tongs to a bucket of cold water or metal bucket with lid – both will snuff out the coals and the wet ones can then be dried out for further use if liked.

If you have a hooded barbecue model simply cover with the hood and close all vents to snuff out the fire-bed.

Everyone hopes their barbecue party will pass without any unfortunate incidents. However, it is always safe to have at hand an assortment of sprays, ointments, dressings and the like, just in case.

In an attempt to keep the party safe, remember not to hang lights or lanterns from trees, or on patio walls or steps where they could easily be pushed over. Keep paper lanterns away from lights and pin down any tablecloths if lights are nearby. In case of an emergency keep a fire-quelling bucket of sand or soil near to hand.

In case of accidents

It is always wise to have a small but comprehensive first-aid kit at hand that contains plasters, antiseptic cream, burn lotion and sting relief. In an effort to reduce the risk of the latter have available a few large repellent sprays or invest in slow-burning 'keep at bay' insect candles to stop the invasion of unwelcome winged visitors.

ACCESSORIES

Basically very few accessories are absolutely essential but several are useful. More frivolous items can be added to the list below if and when required.

Essential accessories for cooking
Long-handled tongs, fork and fish slice for food.

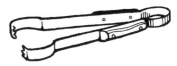

Long-handled tongs for re-arranging, removing or adding coals.

Oven gloves or mittens – the thicker the better.

Long-handled basting brush.

Heavy-duty apron.

Sprinkler bottle or water pistol to douse over exuberant flames.

Heavy-duty aluminium foil.

Aluminium drip pans.

Work surface, table or trolley near barbecue for preparation work and holding flavourings and bastes.

Skewers for kebabs.

Hinged wire flip grill for holding foods which tend to break up easily.

Absorbent kitchen paper and damp cloth for mopping up spills and wiping hands.

Waste bin for the inevitable debris that must be discarded.

Fireproof pots for keeping sauces hot on the edge of the grill.

Essential equipment for serving

Cutlery – plastic if liked.

Plates, bowls etc. – paper if liked.

Glasses – paper or plastic if liked.

Ice bucket for keeping drinks chilled.

Coffee pot for piping hot coffee to conclude the meal.

Can and bottle openers.

Baskets for bread, rolls and toast.

Napkins – again paper if liked.

Condiments – pepper, salt, mustard and relishes.

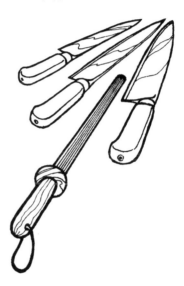

Equipment for cleaning the barbecue

Sturdy wire brush – to brush away debris on the grill rack, do not wash.

Proprietary oven or barbecue cleaner – for end of season cleaning.

Storage

When the barbecue season comes to an end it is important to store or cover the barbecue to prevent rusting or any other harmful effects due to the winter elements.

Ideally clean then wrap a portable model in plastic sheeting (a plastic dustbin bag is good). Metal parts can be smeared with a little petroleum jelly to keep them waterproof if liked.

Outdoor permanent barbecues should be thoroughly cleaned and any metal removable parts should be stored under cover in plastic bags. If not removable then the whole should be wrapped in plastic sheeting and topped with a metal cover – a dustbin lid proves useful but make sure it is securely anchored from blustery winds.

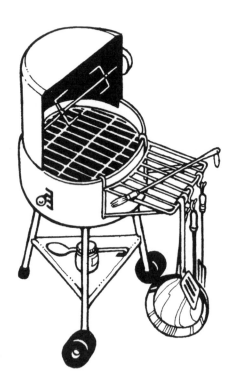

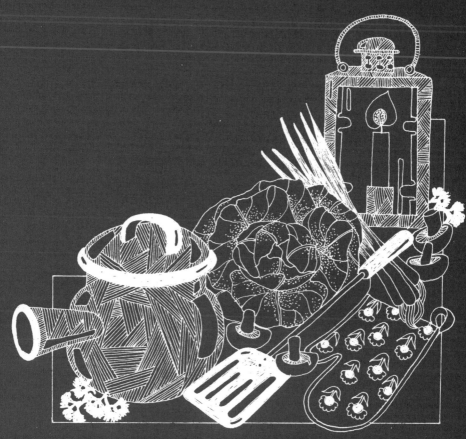

CHOICE OF FOOD

Choice of food

Many different foods, including meat, poultry, fish, vegetables and fruit, are suitable for cooking over charcoal; some need very little preparation and can be barbecued as they are, while others appreciate a little attention like par-cooking, marinating or beating with a meat tenderiser. The golden rule that applies here is to buy the best quality possible – barbecuing will rarely improve the quality, flavour or texture of an inferior, over-ripe or over-mature food.

Meat

Quality is all important when buying meat to barbecue so choose good quality roasting, grilling and frying cuts for most success.

Suitable cuts:

Beef – steaks (rump, fillet and sirloin), hamburgers, topside, thick flank.

Pork – spareribs, loin, leg, fillet, ham and gammon steaks, sausages, frankfurters and chops (loin, chump and sparerib), boneless pieces for kebabs.

Lamb – loin, leg, shoulder, leg steaks, chops (loin and chump), boneless pieces for kebabs.

Veal – fillet, steaks, chops, boneless pieces for kebabs.

Liver

Kidneys

Accompaniments: mustard, horseradish sauce, apple sauce, redcurrant jelly, mint sauce, onion sauce, rosemary jelly, flavoured butters, watercress, grilled tomatoes, crisp onion rings, mushrooms and crisp potatoes.

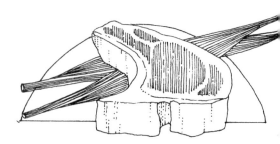

Poultry

Poultry portions are generally more manageable than whole birds for cooking, unless you wish to spit-roast a whole chicken, duck or game bird. Boneless poultry pieces, now sold conveniently cut into bite-sized pieces, prove useful in making speedy kebabs.

Suitable cuts:

Chicken – wings, thighs, quarters, breasts, boneless pieces for kebabs, drumsticks, whole bird (for spit-roasting), chicken burgers.

Duck – quarters, breasts, whole bird (for spit-roasting).

Rabbit – quarters, boneless pieces for kebabs.

Game birds – joints, whole birds (for spit-roasting).

Accompaniments: mustard, bread sauce, redcurrant jelly, flavoured butters, watercress, parsley, grilled tomatoes, mushrooms, crisp potatoes, savoury stuffings.

Fish and Shellfish

Whole fish, fish steaks, fillets and shellfish, if quickly cooked to preserve their succulent flavour, prove splendid barbecue fare. Baste frequently with a complementary sauce or marinade to prevent drying out.

Suitable cuts: fish steaks, cutlets, fillets, whole fish (gutted and cleaned), shellfish (in shell and shelled), crab claws, split lobster.

Accompaniments: lemon and lime slices, savoury butters, parsley, mild mustard, crisp potatoes, savoury stuffings.

Vegetables

There are many vegetables that can be cooked whole over the grill, wrapped in foil or threaded on to skewers and cooked with meat, fish and poultry.

Suitable vegetables: corn, tomatoes, aubergines, onions, potatoes, courgettes, mushrooms, peppers.

Fruit

Fruits need very little cooking, a useful characteristic since they often have to be cooked at the end of the meal after the main high speed cooking has taken place, leaving the fire-bed just warm and glowing.

Suitable fruits: apples, pears, bananas, oranges, peaches, nectarines, pineapple, dates, kumquats, mango, papaya, melon.

COOKING TIMES

Judging when food is cooked is a skill that often comes only with experience. The initial starting temperature of the food, the heat of the grill or coals, the surrounding air temperature and other variables will all influence the cooking speed of food.

The degree to which a food is cooked, whether meat, fish, poultry, vegetable or fruit, will depend upon its thickness, distance from the coals and structure. In order to have varying types of foods cooked at the same time, or the same food cooked to varying degrees of 'doneness' you will need to juggle and alter the distance between the grill and fire-bed during cooking.

Remember to check food constantly and rely upon your own judgement for best results – the grill chart below, however, will give some guidelines.

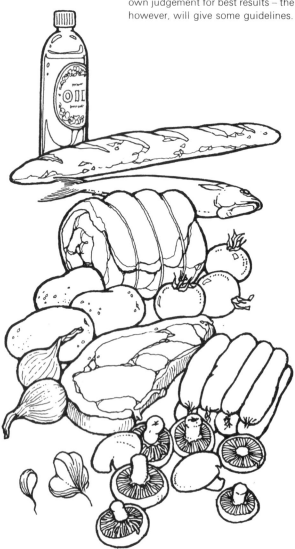

Food	Cut	Size or weight	Coals	Time in minutes
Beef	steaks	2–3 cm/1 inch	hot	8–12 (medium rare)
	hamburger	2–3 cm/1 inch	medium	9–12 (medium)
	kebab		hot	10–15 (medium)
Lamb	chops	2–3 cm/1 inch	medium	10–15 (medium)
	cutlets	2–3 cm/1 inch	medium	7–10 (medium)
	kebab		medium	10–15 (medium)
Pork	chops	2–3 cm/1 inch	medium	15–20
	sausages	large	medium	7–10
	spareribs		medium	60–90
	kebab		medium	15–20
Chicken	quarter		medium	20
	kebab		medium	15–20
	burger		medium	8–12
Duck	portion		medium	20–22
Veal	chops	2–3 cm/1 inch	medium	15–20
	kebab		medium	12–15
Ham	steaks	2–3 cm/1 inch	medium	8–10
	kebab		medium	10–12
Fish and shellfish	steaks	1·5 cm/$\frac{3}{4}$ inch	medium	3–5
	whole, gutted	450 g/1 lb	medium	18–20
		900 g/2 lb	medium	35–45
	fillets	1·5 cm/$\frac{3}{4}$ inch	medium	4–7
	kebab		medium	4-7

COOKING PROCEDURES

Each type of barbecue lends itself better to one or more different cooking procedures – flat cooking on the open grill, spit-roasting, covered grill cooking, skewer cooking or cooking in the coals.

Flat cooking on the open grill

Virtually any food can be cooked flat on the open grill but those thicker than 5 cm/2 inches prove tricky. Steaks, chops and hamburgers are ideal items. To begin cooking, brush the grid with a little oil to prevent sticking, and position about 15 cm/6 inches away from the fire-bed for cooking. Move nearer or further away from the coals as cooking progresses and you have a chance to judge the temperature of the coals.

Spit-roasting

To spit roast on a brazier style barbecue you will need a battery or main line operated spit attachment. Make sure the spit is inserted centrally through the roast or bird for even cooking. If incorrectly balanced the spit will turn jerkily, producing lots of strain on the motor – so much so that it may stop altogether.

The best joints to spit roast are undoubtedly those that have been boned or rolled and birds that have been trussed to a uniform shape. To position the spit place the rod through the centre of the food and tighten the holding forks or tines. Turn it in the palms of your hands to check that it has no tendency to roll in any particular direction. If you have an irregular-shaped piece of meat then consider buying a few balancing weights to counteract the imbalance. Remember too that if you intend to cook a roast with a good fat covering its weight may move during cooking and it may need re-balancing once or twice during the whole cooking operation.

Covered grill cooking

Kettle barbecues and box-shaped or wagon units facilitate covered grill cooking. This type of cooking is ideal for larger and thicker cuts of meat that require long, slow cooking and for foods that need even browning on their surface as well as base, e.g. whole chicken. Ideally cook over a divided bed of coals for foods like these.

Skewer cooking

Skewer cooking is versatile cooking using what you have at hand and is suitable for every type of barbecue. This is the area in which the inventive barbecue chef proves his or her excellence by mixing and matching meat and vegetables, meat and fruit, fish and shellfish and fruit and sweet-toothed offerings. Cook with or without a cover and baste kebabs frequently with savoury sauces, marinades or butters.

In the coals

Some foods can be cooked directly in the fire-bed with excellent results. Corn, aubergines, jacket potatoes, whole onions and whole fruit can be wrapped in a double-thickness piece of heavy-duty foil and placed in the fire-bed to cook like they would in a conventional oven.

Not strictly cooking but certainly aroma-producing as well as flavour-giving is a trick that barbecue enthusiasts often use – throw a few sprigs of fresh herbs on to the hot coals before or during cooking to give a pleasant and scene-setting aroma that guests can appreciate before the delights to come.

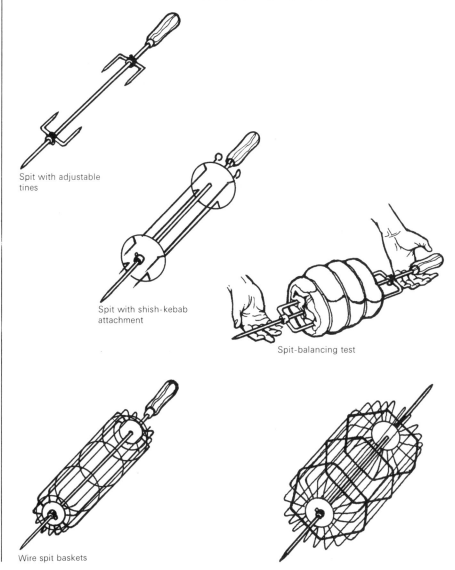

Spit with adjustable tines

Spit with shish-kebab attachment

Spit-balancing test

Wire spit baskets

COOKING AHEAD

Although a barbecue is meant to be an impromptu affair, if you are planning upon a large party it is wise to prepare some of the food beforehand, either complete or ready to reheat. Some food, like vegetable dishes or sauces, can be made in advance or cooked on the barbecue, depending on the grill space and time available.

Precooked food

Appetisers and desserts These are best prepared in advance and kept either in the refrigerator or freezer until required. The simplest dessert, ice cream, can be kept in the freezer right up to the last moment if it is of the soft scoop variety. Keep a stock of sweet sauces and whipped cream to go with it.

Salads These can be washed and prepared beforehand and kept chilled in the refrigerator until required.

Dressings Can be prepared well in advance and stored in a screw-topped jar. Before using, simply shake for 10 seconds to mix.

Meat Steak is spoilt by reheating but you can go a long way towards taking the load off your grill by pre-browning and pre-cooking items such as chicken portions, lamb and pork chops and sausages, then simply finishing the cooking and crisping on the barbecue itself.

Food from the freezer

Think of your freezer as a store-cupboard and you won't go far wrong. The weather hardly ever turns out to plan, so make sure you have a stock of steaks, chops, chicken portions, sausages, vegetables and bread ready for when the weather is kind.

Use it to store appetisers and desserts made well in advance of your barbecue party, as well as a stock of commercially prepared desserts such as cheesecakes, gâteaux and iced cakes.

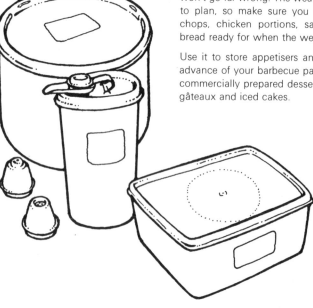

KEEPING FOOD HOT

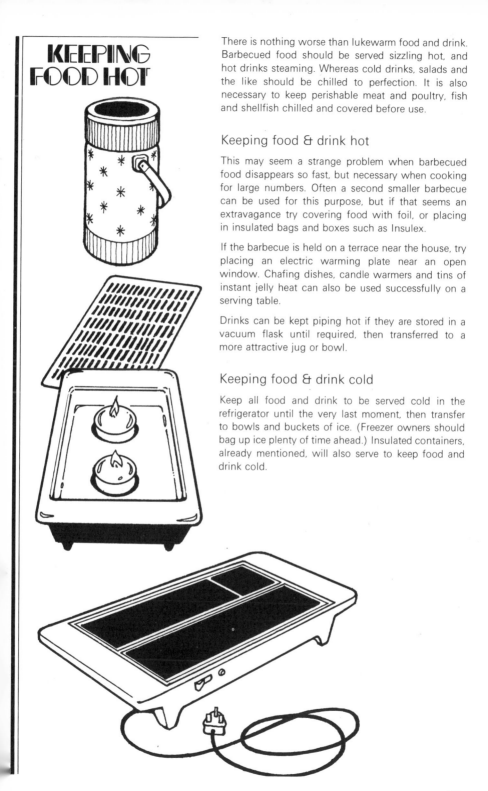

There is nothing worse than lukewarm food and drink. Barbecued food should be served sizzling hot, and hot drinks steaming. Whereas cold drinks, salads and the like should be chilled to perfection. It is also necessary to keep perishable meat and poultry, fish and shellfish chilled and covered before use.

Keeping food & drink hot

This may seem a strange problem when barbecued food disappears so fast, but necessary when cooking for large numbers. Often a second smaller barbecue can be used for this purpose, but if that seems an extravagance try covering food with foil, or placing in insulated bags and boxes such as Insulex.

If the barbecue is held on a terrace near the house, try placing an electric warming plate near an open window. Chafing dishes, candle warmers and tins of instant jelly heat can also be used successfully on a serving table.

Drinks can be kept piping hot if they are stored in a vacuum flask until required, then transferred to a more attractive jug or bowl.

Keeping food & drink cold

Keep all food and drink to be served cold in the refrigerator until the very last moment, then transfer to bowls and buckets of ice. (Freezer owners should bag up ice plenty of time ahead.) Insulated containers, already mentioned, will also serve to keep food and drink cold.

FLAVOURINGS

Flavourings are all important to a barbecue meal. Even though plain grilled meat, poultry, fish and shellfish are delicious in themselves, combined with a complementary flavouring they taste even better.

To satisfy all tastes, supply a large range of herbs, spices, sauces and dressings for guests to help themselves.

Herbs

Sprinkle on plain grilled meat, poultry, fish and shellfish, and on to coals to impart a delicious flavour and aroma to the same. Wherever possible try to use fresh herbs, but substitute good quality dried if this is not possible.

Add herbs to dressings and marinades as far ahead as possible, giving them plenty of time to fully flavour.

Bags of bouquet garni, secured on the end of a skewer, stick or fork, can be dipped in butter, oil or marinade; used as a basting brush will give food being cooked a delicate but recognisable herb flavour.

Spices and seasonings

Everyday spices and seasonings are excellent for flavouring barbecued food, but there are several specially prepared barbecue seasonings on the market which will give the right hot and spicy flavour to barbecued food.

Barbecued mackerel with dill (see recipe page 63), gooseberry herb sauce (see recipe page 94) and cucumber relish (see recipe page 103)

BARBECUE PARTIES

One of the prime advantages of moving a party outside the confines of the house is the opportunity it offers you to entertain a large number of people at one time — many more than you would be able to serve comfortably indoors. And this is where the barbecue party comes into its own. From informal to grand, the mood can be what you choose to make it.

Such a party calls for the same kind of planning that goes into any party — but on a bigger scale. Since you will have more guests, you will need more food, more help and probably more cooking equipment. One of the cheapest and most efficient ways of doing this is to pool equipment. Ask some of your guests to bring along their barbecues and then put them in charge of that grill. So while some are grilling meats or basting roasts, others can be tending to the vegetables, appetisers or desserts.

If you opt to do the complete party yourself, a buffet or help-yourself meal will be the easiest to manage. But whatever option you take, your party will still need careful planning.

Planning the menu

If at all possible suit the meal to the weather. On a cold day provide plenty of hot meats, spicy hot sauces, warm bread and steaming hot drinks. On a hot day, cool dishes like salads and fruit dishes will be very popular, with simple cooked meat or fish.

Choose the menu to suit the guests, too. If there are lots of children around provide plenty of finger food such as sausages, fish fingers and chicken drumsticks. For a smaller, informal gathering be more adventurous with steaks and fish and special desserts. For a large party, variety is the keyword.

Always try to serve food that is easy to handle, and keep to one main kind of meat or fish, unless it is a large gathering. Accompany with a salad and one or two vegetables, plenty of bread of different varieties, drinks and a dessert.

Quantities

An often quoted rule is to think of average indoor helpings and then to double them. Keep this in mind and you won't go far wrong. Appetites are large in the open air when the atmosphere is relaxed and food can be seen and smelt to be cooking.

Be just as generous with drinks. These will vary with the weather too; long cool drinks being popular on a hot day, warm coffee, mulled wine and spirit-based drinks being preferable on a cold.

Grilled steaks, mixed grill kebabs (see recipe page 51) and oil-wrapped jacket potatoes

Party pointers

Have plenty of everything — fire and food alike. Fresh air sharpens appetites. Leftovers can be used another day, but nothing will save a meal that is too little and too late.

Expect the unexpected. Have some plan worked out in case a sudden summer storm blows up. Move the guests to the porch or house. If your grill is portable, find a safe, well-ventilated place where you can move it. On a patio, a huge sun umbrella or makeshift canvas covering will protect the fire and the cook.

Make some arrangements for throwing a little light on the situation. Dusk quickly turns to dark.

Be prepared to cope with barbecue enemies — flies, ants and moths. There are many pest deterrents on the market.

Develop a definite plan for a clean-up. Scrape and stack plates in an orderly fashion, then carry them into the kitchen. You will want to spend what is left of the evening in a pleasant atmosphere.

APPETISERS

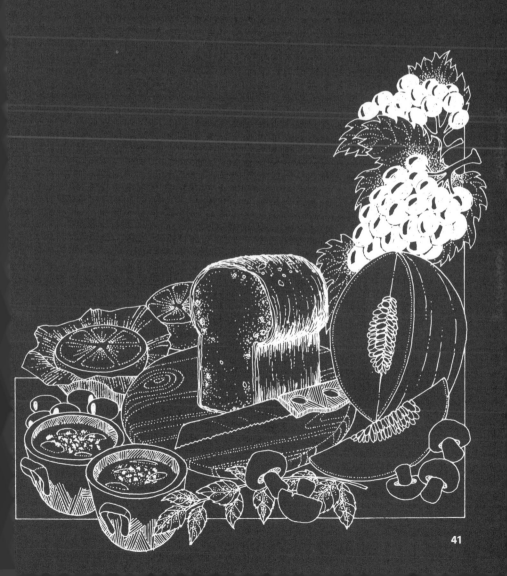

Blue cheese dip

Makes 150 g/5 oz

METRIC/IMPERIAL
100 g/4 oz Danish Blue cheese, softened
2 tablespoons single cream
6 large pecan nuts, finely crushed
1½ tablespoons finely chopped chives

Combine all the ingredients in a medium mixing bowl, beating with a wooden spoon until they are well blended. Serve at room temperature.

Spicy cheese and brandy dip

Makes 450 g/1 lb

METRIC/IMPERIAL
275 g/10 oz Cheddar cheese, grated
75 g/3 oz butter
175 ml/6 fl oz single cream
½ teaspoon Tabasco sauce
4½ tablespoons brandy

Cream the cheese and butter together in a medium mixing bowl with a wooden spoon. Gradually beat in the cream, then the Tabasco sauce and brandy, beating until the mixture is smooth and thick. Serve at room temperature.

Crudités

METRIC/IMPERIAL
carrots
celery sticks
green and red peppers
cucumber
cauliflower
small tomatoes
spring onions
button mushrooms
chicory
radishes

Wash, trim and dry all of the vegetables. Cut the carrots, celery, green and red peppers and cucumber into thin strips. Separate the cauliflower into florets. Leave the tomatoes, spring onions and button mushrooms whole. Separate the chicory into leaves and cut the radishes into roses. Arrange on a large platter.

Serve with sea salt, ground black pepper and blue cheese dip or spicy cheese and brandy dip (see above).

Grilled grapefruit

METRIC/IMPERIAL
3 large grapefruit
3 tablespoons sherry (optional)
3 tablespoons honey or brown sugar
6 maraschino cherries

Cooking time
15 minutes
Serves 6

Cut each grapefruit in half, cutting loose the segments and removing pips. Place each half on a double thickness of aluminium foil and spoon about a half tablespoon of sherry and honey or brown sugar over it. Wrap the edges of the foil securely to enclose.

Cook on the grill, over medium coals, cut side up, for about 15 minutes. Remove, unwrap and top each grapefruit half with a maraschino cherry. Serve at once.

Gazpacho

Serves 4–6

METRIC/IMPERIAL
3 slices brown bread, cut into cubes
300 ml/$\frac{1}{2}$ pint canned tomato juice
2 cloves garlic, finely chopped
$\frac{1}{2}$ cucumber, peeled and finely chopped
1 green pepper, deseeded and chopped
1 red pepper, deseeded and chopped
1 medium onion, finely chopped
675 g/1$\frac{1}{2}$ lb tomatoes, peeled, deseeded and chopped
4$\frac{1}{2}$ tablespoons olive oil
2 tablespoons red wine vinegar
$\frac{1}{2}$ teaspoon salt
$\frac{1}{4}$ teaspoon black pepper
$\frac{1}{2}$ teaspoon marjoram

Place the bread cubes in a medium mixing bowl and pour over the tomato juice. Leave to soak for 5 minutes, then squeeze carefully to extract the excess juice. Transfer the soaked bread to a larger mixing bowl, reserving the juice.

Add the garlic, cucumber, peppers, onion and tomatoes to the bread and stir well to mix. Purée the ingredients together, either through a sieve or in the liquidiser. Stir in the reserved tomato juice. Add the oil, vinegar, salt, pepper and marjoram. Stir well to blend. Turn the soup into a deep tureen or serving dish and chill for at least 1 hour before serving.

Serve with bowls of chopped onion, peppers, cucumber and toasted bread croûtons.

Potted shrimps or prawns

METRIC/IMPERIAL

Serves 4

50 g/2 oz butter
⅛ teaspoon ground mace
pinch of cayenne pepper
¼ teaspoon salt
¼ teaspoon black pepper
225 g/8 oz cooked shrimps or prawns
50 g/2 oz clarified butter, melted

In a large frying pan, melt the butter over moderate heat. When the foam subsides, stir in the mace, cayenne and seasoning. Add the shrimps or prawns and coat them thoroughly with the seasoned butter. Remove from the heat.

Spoon equal amounts of the mixture into four small pots, leaving a 5-mm/¼-inch headspace at the top. Pour 1 tablespoon of the clarified butter into each pot. Cover with foil and chill for 2 hours.

Remove from the refrigerator, discard foil and serve with brown bread and butter.

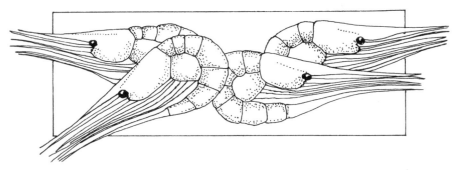

Kipper pâté

METRIC/IMPERIAL

Cooking time
10–15 minutes
Serves 4

175 g/6 oz frozen buttered kipper fillets
40 g/1½ oz butter, softened
black pepper
grated nutmeg

Cook the kipper fillets as directed on the packet and turn the contents, including the juices, into a mixing bowl. Remove any skin and bone then mince or pound the kipper until quite smooth. Beat in the butter and season to taste with pepper and nutmeg. Turn into a small dish and chill before serving.

Serve with brown bread or crispbread.

Stilton pâté

Cooking time
20 minutes
Serves 8

METRIC/IMPERIAL
750 ml/1¼ pints milk
1 large onion, coarsely chopped
1 carrot, chopped
2 stalks celery, chopped
bouquet garni
75 g/3 oz butter
75 g/3 oz flour
3 tablespoons mayonnaise
2 teaspoons lemon juice
3 cloves garlic, crushed
10 stuffed olives, finely chopped
½ teaspoon salt
½ teaspoon black pepper
pinch of cayenne pepper
350 g/12 oz Stilton cheese, rind removed and crumbled

Pour the milk into a saucepan set over a high heat. Bring to the boil, reduce the heat and add the onion, carrot, celery and bouquet garni. Cover and simmer for 15 minutes. Remove from the heat and cool. Pour through a strainer into a large bowl, pressing the vegetables to extract any juice.

In a medium saucepan, melt the butter. Stir in the flour to make a smooth paste. Gradually add the milk, stirring constantly. Return to the heat and cook for 2–3 minutes, stirring, until the sauce is very thick and smooth. Set aside to cool to room temperature.

When the sauce is cool, beat in the mayonnaise, lemon juice, garlic and olives, and season with the salt, pepper and cayenne. Sieve the cheese into the mixture and beat until smooth.

Spoon into a serving dish and smooth the surface. Place in the refrigerator to chill for 1 hour before serving. Serve with hot buttered toast or rolls.

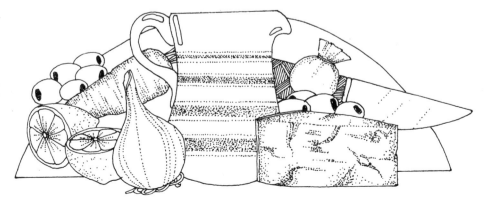

Melon boats

METRIC/IMPERIAL
2 small honeydew or ogen melons
2 pears, peeled, cored and chopped
100 g/4 oz black grapes, halved and pipped
2 teaspoons lemon juice
3 tablespoons clear honey
4 sprigs of mint

Cut the melons in half and remove the seeds. Using a small spoon or melon baller, scoop out the melon flesh in balls.

Transfer to a mixing bowl. Add the pears and grapes. Stir in the lemon juice and honey.

Scallop the edges of the melon halves with a sharp knife. Pile the fruit mixture back into the melon boats and chill for 20 minutes.

Just before serving, garnish each boat with a sprig of mint.

Mushrooms à la grecque

Cooking time
15 minutes
Serves 4

METRIC/IMPERIAL
25 g/1 oz onion, grated
2 tablespoons olive oil
200 ml/7 fl oz dry white wine
bouquet garni
1 clove garlic, peeled
salt and black pepper
350 g/12 oz button mushrooms
225 g/8 oz tomatoes, peeled
Garnish
chopped parsley

Sauté the onion in the oil until soft and transparent. Add the wine, bouquet garni and garlic. Season to taste with salt and black pepper.

Wipe the mushrooms clean but leave whole. Add to the onion mixture with the quartered and deseeded tomatoes. Cook gently, covered, for 5 minutes, then uncover for 5 more minutes to reduce the liquid by half. Remove from the heat and allow to cool. Remove the bouquet garni and garlic. Serve chilled in individual dishes sprinkled with chopped parsley.

MEAT, POULTRY AND GAME

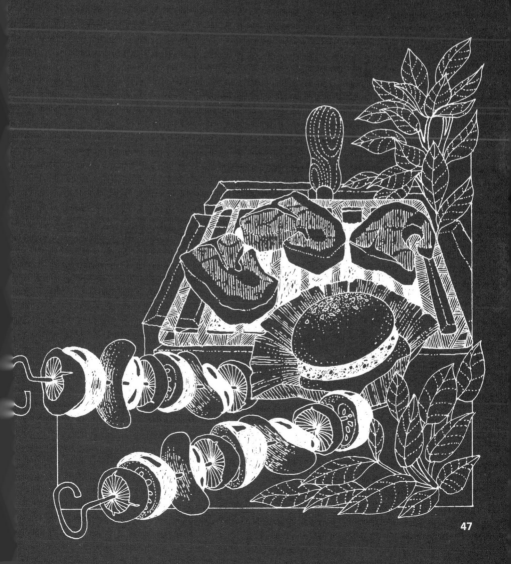

Steak au poivre

METRIC/IMPERIAL
2 tablespooons black peppercorns
4 (150-g/5-oz) rump or fillet steaks
salt
50 g/2 oz butter
2 tablespoons brandy
150 ml/¼ pint double cream

Cooking time
6–10 minutes
Serves 4

Illustrated on pages 66–67

Crush half the peppercorns and rub into both sides of the steaks. Season to taste with salt.

Melt the butter in a frying pan over hot coals. Add the steaks and fry quickly on both sides for about 6-10 minutes, until well browned and cooked according to taste.

Pour over the brandy, ignite, remove from the heat and allow the flames to die down. Arrange the steaks on a warmed serving plate.

Stir the cream into the pan juices and cook for 1 minute, stirring continuously. Add the remaining peppercorns, blending well. Spoon over the steaks and serve at once.

Chicken burgers with devilled pineapple relish

METRIC/IMPERIAL
350 g/12 oz skinned and boneless chicken breast, finely chopped or minced
350 g/12 oz sausagemeat
salt and pepper
Relish
1 tomato, peeled and finely chopped
½ medium red or green pepper, cored, deseeded and finely chopped
6 tablespoons well-drained, canned crushed pineapple
1 tablespoon mild prepared mustard

Cooking time
7–8 minutes
Serves 4–8

Mix the chicken with the sausagemeat and salt and pepper to taste. Using floured hands, shape the mixture into eight burgers.

Place directly on the grill and cook, over medium coals, for 8–12 minutes, turning once.

Meanwhile to make the relish, mix the tomato with the pepper, pineapple and mustard, blending well.

Serve the hot cooked burgers with a little of the devilled pineapple relish.

Hamburgers

METRIC/IMPERIAL
675 g/1½ lb lean minced beef
25 g/1 oz fresh breadcrumbs
½ teaspoon salt
¼ teaspoon black pepper
¼ teaspoon dried thyme
1 small egg, lightly beaten
4 hamburger or large soft buns
40 g/1½ oz butter
4 lettuce leaves
2 small tomatoes, thinly sliced
1 small onion, sliced into rings

Cooking time
10–12 minutes
Serves 4

Place the beef, breadcrumbs, salt, pepper, thyme and beaten egg in a bowl. Mix thoroughly to blend. Divide the mixture into four equal portions and shape each into a patty or hamburger shape.

Place directly on the grill and cook, over medium coals, for about 5–6 minutes each side.

Split the hamburger buns in half and butter each half. Place a lettuce leaf on the base of each bun half. Top with a hamburger, a few slices of tomato, a few onion rings and the bun lid. Serve at once.

Variation
Onion burgers (illustrated on page 95). Prepare and cook as above but omit the tomato and onion rings. Melt 25 g/1 oz butter in a small pan. Add 1 large onion, sliced into rings. Cook until just softened, about 5–10 minutes. Spoon on top of the burgers just before the end of the cooking time.

Lamb's liver and bacon skewers

METRIC/IMPERIAL
350 g/12 oz lamb's liver, cut into bite-sized pieces
100g/4 oz rindless bacon, halved and rolled
100 g/4 oz small button mushrooms, wiped
50 g/2 oz butter, melted
pepper

Cooking time
8–10 minutes
Serves 4

Thread the lamb's liver, bacon and mushrooms alternately on to four large skewers.

Brush with the butter and season well with pepper. Cook over medium to low coals for 8–10 minutes, turning frequently.

Serve hot with warm pitta bread and a seasonal salad.

Chilli beef chowder

METRIC/IMPERIAL
675 g/1½ lb braising steak
4 medium potatoes
225 g/8 oz carrots
2 onions
1 green pepper
1 clove garlic
salt and black pepper
1 tablespoon oil
2 teaspoons chilli powder
1 (227-g/8-oz) can tomatoes
1 (432-g/15¼-oz) can red kidney beans
1 tablespoon tomato puree
1·15 litres/2 pints beef stock
1 tablespoon flour

Cooking time
1¼ hours
Serves 6

Illustrated on page 56

Trim and discard any excess fat from the beef and cut into bite-sized cubes. Peel and dice the potatoes. Peel and finely dice the carrots and onions. Slice off 6 thin rings from the pepper and reserve. Cut the remainder into small dice, discarding seeds and pith. Peel and crush the garlic to a smooth paste with a little salt.

Heat the oil in a large, heavy-based pan and add the meat, vegetables and garlic. Fry for 3 minutes. Stir in the chilli powder and fry for 1 minute. Stir in the tomatoes, drained kidney beans, tomato purée, seasoning to taste, and stock. Bring to the boil, reduce heat, cover and simmer very gently for 45 minutes over low coals. Mix the flour with a little water to form a smooth paste. Stir into the chowder and continue cooking for a few more minutes, until thick.

Garnish the soup with the reserved pepper rings just before serving with wholemeal bread or rolls.

Orange-glazed pork loin

METRIC/IMPERIAL
1 (1·5–2·5-kg/3–5-lb) loin of pork
Sauce and glaze
40 g/1½ oz butter
100 g/4 oz brown sugar
1 (178-ml/6¼-fl oz) can frozen concentrated orange juice
4½ tablespoons water
2 teaspoons cornflour
100 g/4 oz green grapes, halved and pipped

Cooking time
1¼–2½ hours
Serves 6–8

Score the fat on the pork loin at 2·5-cm/1-inch intervals. Place the meat, fat side up, on the grill and cook over low coals, allowing 25–30 minutes per half kilo/per lb. Turn from time to time during cooking.

Meanwhile, heat the butter in a medium saucepan. Stir in the brown sugar. Add the concentrated orange juice and stir until smooth. Remove a little of this sauce to use as a baste for the pork. Stir the water into the cornflour and add gradually to the remaining orange sauce. Cook, stirring constantly, until the sauce thickens. Cook for a further 8 minutes. Add the grapes and serve with the pork.

Sweet and sour spareribs

METRIC/IMPERIAL
900 g/2 lb spareribs
Sauce
150 ml/¼ pint cider vinegar
2 teaspoons made mustard
3 tablespoons light muscovado sugar
3 tablespoons Worcestershire sauce
5 tablespoons tomato purée
3 tablespoons lemon juice
1 small onion, finely chopped
salt and pepper

Cooking time
1–1 hours
Serves 4

Place all the sauce ingredients in a pan. Bring to the boil, lower the heat and simmer for 30 minutes, stirring occasionally.

Using a sharp pointed knife, make deep slits in the spareribs and brush with the sweet and sour sauce.

Place directly on the grill and cook for 1–1 hours, turning frequently and basting occasionally with the sauce. Serve with any of the remaining sauce.

Mixed grill kebabs

METRIC/IMPERIAL
8 lamb's kidneys
8 mushrooms
4 small tomatoes
8 small pork sausages
olive oil
salt and black pepper

Cooking time
15–20 minutes
Serves 4

Illustrated on page 38

Skin and halve the kidneys, removing cores. Wipe the mushrooms. Halve the tomatoes.

Thread the sausages, kidneys, mushrooms and tomatoes alternately on skewers. Brush with oil, season well and cook over low coals for about 15–20 minutes. Turn from time to time. Serve with a green salad and jacket potatoes.

Summer lamb parcels

Cooking time
30 minutes
Serves 4

METRIC/IMPERIAL
4 lamb leg steaks
salt and pepper
2 onions, sliced
100 g/4 oz mature English Cheddar cheese, sliced
1 tablespoon chopped parsley

Cut four pieces of aluminium foil large enough to enclose each leg steak. Place a steak in the centre of each and season with salt and pepper to taste.

Divide the onion between the steaks and top each with an equal quantity of the sliced cheese. Seal the edges of the foil to make parcels.

Place on the grill, over medium coals, and cook for 30 minutes, turning twice.

Remove the meat from the foil parcels to serve. Sprinkle liberally with the chopped parsley.

Serve hot with jacket potatoes or crusty bread and a salad.

Skewered lamb meatballs

Cooking time
15–20 minutes
Serves 6

METRIC/IMPERIAL
100 g/4 oz sultanas
675 g/1½ lb boned shoulder of lamb
225 g/8 oz fresh white breadcrumbs
2 eggs, beaten
salt and black pepper
1 tablespoon curry powder
2 onions, sliced into rings

Illustrated on page 78

Soak the sultanas in water for 1 hour. Drain. Mince the lamb and mix with the breadcrumbs, sultanas, beaten eggs, seasoning and curry powder. Mix well together then shape into 12 meatballs. Arrange on to six skewers alternately with the onion rings. Grill, over hot coals, for 15–20 minutes, turning. Serve on a bed of outdoor pilaf (see page 79).

Note: Traditionally, these meatballs are enclosed in a caul before grilling, which your butcher may be able to supply, but this is optional.

Skewered noisettes of lamb

METRIC/IMPERIAL
4 noisettes of lamb
2 teaspoons made mustard
1 clove garlic, chopped
few sprigs of rosemary, crushed
8 shallots or small onions
8 small tomatoes
olive oil
salt and black pepper

Cooking time
30 minutes
Serves 4

Illustrated on page 19

Trim the noisettes of lamb and spread the mustard lightly on each side. Sprinkle with a little chopped garlic and crushed rosemary.

Peel and parboil the onions until almost tender. Thread on to skewers with the lamb noisettes and tomatoes. Brush with oil and season with salt and pepper. Grill over medium coals for 30 minutes, turning from time to time.

Serve with boiled rice and special barbecue sauce (see page 92).

Minted leg of lamb

METRIC/IMPERIAL
1 (1·75 kg–2·25-kg/4–5-lb) leg of lamb, boned and rolled
mint leaves
Marinade
50 g/2 oz brown sugar
3 tablespoons salad oil
1 teaspoon grated lemon rind
3 tablespoons lemon juice
3 tablespoons vinegar
4 tablespoons chopped mint leaves
1 teaspoon chopped tarragon leaves
1 teaspoon salt
1 teaspoon dry mustard

Cooking time
1¼–2 hours
Serves 6–8

Mix together the ingredients for the marinade. Heat to boiling, reduce heat and simmer for 5 minutes. Cool. Place the lamb in a plastic bag or shallow dish. Pour the cooled marinade over the meat and leave to marinate for 24 hours.

Cook over medium coals, allowing 20–25 minutes per half kilo/per lb. During cooking baste with the marinade and throw fresh mint leaves on to the coals to give the lamb a delicious flavour and aroma.

Veal chops with Roquefort and mushroom stuffing

METRIC/IMPERIAL
4 veal chops
1 tablespoon olive oil
Stuffing
75 g/3 oz bacon rashers
100 g/4 oz button mushrooms
1 medium onion
50 g/2 oz Roquefort cheese, crumbled
50 g/2 oz parsley, chopped
salt and black pepper

Cooking time
35–40 minutes
Serves 4

Illustrated opposite

Cut the bacon into small dice and place in a saucepan. Heat gently until the fat runs, then add the cleaned and sliced mushrooms, chopped onion and a little oil if the mixture seems too dry. Cook for 2–3 minutes. Remove from the heat, allow to cool slightly then mix in the cheese, parsley and seasoning to taste.

Make a slit in each chop and place in the stuffing. Brush on both sides with the oil then secure each slit with wooden toothpicks or cocktail sticks. Place on the grill and cook over medium coals for 30 minutes, turning once. Remove cocktail sticks before serving with a crisp salad and crusty bread.

Note: If unable to obtain Roquefort, substitute Stilton or another good blue cheese.

Veal chops with Kirsch

METRIC/IMPERIAL
4 veal chops
1 tablespoon olive oil
salt and black pepper
3 tablespoons Kirsch
juice of 1 orange
chopped parsley

Cooking time
18–24 minutes
Serves 4

Brush the chops with the oil and season well on both sides. Grill over medium coals for 9–12 minutes on each side, until cooked. Place on a warmed serving dish.

Warm the Kirsch and pour over the veal chops. Ignite. When the flames die down add the orange juice and a little chopped parsley.

Veal chops with Roquefort and mushroom stuffing (see recipe above)

Bacon-wrapped sausages

METRIC/IMPERIAL
450 g/1 lb pork sausages
100 g/4 oz Cheddar cheese, sliced
8 rashers bacon
4 teaspoons made mustard

Cooking time
20 minutes
Serves 4

Illustrated on page 95

Barbecue the sausages over medium coals for about 15 minutes, then slit them lengthways, almost through. Fill with the cheese slices and press the sausages together again.

Spread the bacon rashers with mustard and wrap around the sausages, securing the ends with wooden cocktail sticks. Place on the grill again and cook over medium coals for a further 5 minutes, or until the cheese melts and the bacon is crisp. Serve with a mixed green salad and potato crisps.

Hot dogs

METRIC/IMPERIAL
4 large frankfurter sausages
4 long bread rolls or pieces of French bread
4 tablespoons tomato ketchup (optional)

Cooking time
5–8 minutes
Serves 4
Illustrated opposite

Lightly prick the frankfurters. Place directly on the grill and cook, over medium coals, for 5–8 minutes, turning frequently.

Place the bread rolls on a board and cut carefully without going right through the bread, leaving it 'hinged' at the back.

Using tongs or a fork, place a frankfurter in each roll. Spoon over a little of the tomato ketchup, if liked. Serve in soft paper napkins while still warm.

Hot dogs (see recipe above) and chilli beef chowder
(see recipe page 50)

Spicy ham steaks

METRIC/IMPERIAL

4 ham or gammon steaks, 2·5-cm/1-inch thick
4 pineapple slices
Marinade
150 ml/¼ pint sherry
150 ml/¼ pint pineapple juice
2 tablespoons salad oil
pinch of ground cloves
1 tablespoon dry mustard
4 tablespoons brown sugar
1 teaspoon paprika pepper

Cooking time
20 minutes
Serves 4

Snip along the edges of the ham steaks to prevent them curling up. Mix all the ingredients for the marinade together. Marinate the ham for 2–3 hours, turning occasionally.

Remove the ham from the marinade and grill over low to medium coals for about 20 minutes, basting with the remaining marinade from time to time.

Serve hot topped with the slices of pineapple.

Devilled chicken

METRIC/IMPERIAL

4 large chicken portions
2 teaspoons salt
2 teaspoons sugar
1 teaspoon pepper
1 teaspoon ground ginger
1 teaspoon dry mustard
½ teaspoon curry powder
50 g/2 oz butter
Baste
2 tablespoons tomato ketchup
1 tablespoon mushroom ketchup
1 tablespoon Worcestershire sauce
1 tablespoon soy sauce
1 tablespoon plum jam
dash of Tabasco sauce

Cooking time
30 minutes
Serves 4

Place the chicken portions in a large shallow dish. Mix together the salt, sugar, pepper, ginger, mustard and curry powder and rub into the chicken. Leave for 1 hour.

Melt the butter and brush over the chicken. Grill for 20 minutes, over medium coals, until crisp, turning.

Mix the remaining ingredients together and any remaining butter. Heat gently and use to baste the chicken. Cook for a further 10 minutes, basting with this sauce from time to time. Heat any remaining sauce and serve with the chicken.

Barbecued rosemary chicken

METRIC/IMPERIAL
4 chicken quarters
sprigs of rosemary
Glaze
4 tablespoons vinegar
1 tablespoon molasses sugar
1 tablespoon Worcestershire sauce
1 tablespoon tomato purée
1 teaspoon paprika pepper
1 small onion, finely chopped
salt and pepper

Cooking time
35–45 minutes
Serves 4

Illustrated on page 20

Place the vinegar, sugar, Worcestershire sauce, tomato purée, paprika, onion and seasoning to taste in a small pan. Bring to the boil, lower the heat and simmer for 10 minutes.

Wash and dry the chicken quarters. Brush with the glaze to coat. Place directly on the grill and cook over medium coals for 20–25 minutes, turning occasionally and basting frequently with the glaze. About 10 minutes before the end of the cooking time add a few sprigs of fresh rosemary to the coals and the chicken for an aromatic flavour.

Serve hot with grilled tomatoes and orange and lemon barbecue sauce (see page 92).

Barbecued chicken drumsticks

METRIC/IMPERIAL
8 chicken drumsticks
Baste
50 g/2 oz butter
1 onion, grated
1 (227-g/8-oz) can tomatoes
2 tablespoons Worcestershire sauce
25 g/1 oz demerara sugar
1 teaspoon salt
black pepper

Cooking time
50 minutes
Serves 4

Trim away any excess skin from the drumsticks. Combine all the baste ingredients in a small saucepan, cover and simmer for 30 minutes. Rub through a sieve or liquidise until smooth.

Brush the drumsticks with the glaze and cook, over medium coals, for 10 minutes. Turn and cook for a further 10 minutes. Brush with the baste several times during cooking. Heat any remaining baste and serve with the chicken drumsticks.

Chinese duckling

Cooking time
45–60 minutes
Serves 2–4

METRIC/IMPERIAL
1 duckling
2 egg yolks
2 tablespoons soy sauce
3 tablespoons honey

Depending upon the size of the duckling, split in half or divide into quarters. Rub with a mixture of the egg yolks, soy sauce and honey.

Grill, cut side down, for 45–60 minutes, over medium to low coals, turning from time to time. Towards the end of the cooking time raise the heat to crisp the skin.

Skewered rabbit with mustard

Cooking time
15 minutes
Serves 4

METRIC/IMPERIAL
450 g/1 lb boneless rabbit meat
salt and pepper
4 teaspoons made mustard
4 teaspoons olive oil

Illustrated on page 96

Trim and cut the rabbit meat into serving-size pieces. Thread on to skewers and season with salt and pepper. Brush lightly with the mustard and then with the oil.

Barbecue, over medium to hot coals, for 15 minutes, turning from time to time. Serve with additional mustard sauce (see page 97) and jacket potatoes.

Note: For those guests who do not like mustard substitute redcurrant jelly for this.

FISH AND SHELLFISH

Grilled marinated sardines

METRIC/IMPERIAL
12 fresh sardines, cleaned
Marinade
2 tablespoons lemon juice
3 tablespoons cider vinegar
1 tablespoon clear honey
1 tablespoon oil
150 ml/¼ pint dry cider

Cooking time
8–10 minutes
Serves 4

Illustrated on page 113

Place the sardines in a shallow dish. Make the marinade by beating the lemon juice with the vinegar, honey, oil and cider, blending well. Pour over the sardines, cover and leave to marinate in the refrigerator for 2–3 hours, turning occasionally.

Remove the sardines with a slotted spoon and place directly on the grill, or in a grill rack, and cook over hot coals for 8–10 minutes, turning once. Baste from time to time with the marinade.

Serve hot with chive or green butter (see pages 106 and 107) and a dish of ratatouille (see page 80).

Barbecued salmon trout with orange dressing

METRIC/IMPERIAL
1 whole salmon trout, weighing 1·4–1·5 kg/3–3½ lb,
  cleaned and gutted
3 tablespoons orange juice
grated rind and juice of 1 lemon
salt and pepper
Dressing
150 ml/¼ pint mayonnaise
150 ml/¼ pint set natural yogurt
1–2 tablespoons orange juice
Garnish
sprigs of watercress

Cooking time
1–1¼ hours
Serves 6

Place the salmon trout on a large double-thickness piece of aluminium foil. Pour the orange juice, grated lemon rind and juice over the fish. Season with salt and pepper to taste. Wrap up securely to enclose.

Place directly on to the grill and cook over medium coals for 1–1¼ hours, turning occasionally.

Meanwhile to make the dressing, mix the mayonnaise with the yogurt, orange juice and seasoning to taste, blending well.

Serve the cooked salmon trout garnished with watercress sprigs and accompany with the orange dressing.

Baked stuffed fish

METRIC/IMPERIAL

1 whole cod, haddock or salmon, weighing 1·25–1·5 kg/2½–3 lb
Stuffing
1 onion, chopped
2 sticks celery, chopped
3 rashers bacon, chopped and fried until crisp
2 tablespoons chopped parsley
40 g/1½ oz fresh white breadcrumbs
50 g/2 oz butter, melted
salt and black pepper

Cooking time
1–1¼ hours
Serves 4–6

Clean and gut the fish, removing the head if desired. Mix the stuffing ingredients together and place in the cavity of the fish, closing the opening with wooden cocktail sticks. Place on a large piece of buttered foil, season well, then wrap up securely.

Cook over medium coals for 1–1¼ hours, or until the fish flakes easily with a fork. Turn from time to time during cooking.

Barbecued mackerel with dill

METRIC/IMPERIAL

4 medium mackerel
2 tablespoons salad oil
juice of 1 lemon
salt and black pepper
sprigs of dill
gooseberry herb sauce (see page 94)
cucumber relish (see page 103)

Cooking time
20 minutes
Serves 4

Illustrated on page 37

Clean the mackerel, removing the heads if desired. Slash the flesh diagonally on each side of the fish about three times. Brush with the oil and lemon juice. Season to taste and scatter with the sprigs of dill.

Grill over medium coals for 10 minutes on each side, turning once and brushing from time to time with the oil and lemon juice. Serve with gooseberry herb sauce and cucumber relish.

Skewered plaice

METRIC/IMPERIAL
12 rashers streaky bacon
450 g/1 lb plaice fillets
150 ml/¼ pint cider and honey marinade (see page 99)
lemon sauce (see page 94)

Cooking time
10 minutes
Serves 4

Illustrated opposite

Place the bacon rashers on a board and stretch with the back of a round-bladed knife. Cut each rasher in half. Remove the skin from the plaice fillets and divide into 24 pieces. Place each on a halved rasher of bacon and roll up. Secure with a wooden cocktail stick. Place in a dish with the cider and honey marinade and leave to marinate for 2 hours.

Remove from the marinade, remove cocktail sticks and place on four skewers. Grill on the barbecue, over medium coals, for 8–10 minutes, turning and brushing from time to time with the marinade. Serve hot with lemon sauce and crusty bread.

Marinated salmon steaks with capers

METRIC/IMPERIAL
6 individual salmon steaks
Marinade
6 tablespoons capers
4 tablespoons olive oil
juice of 1 lemon
1 small onion, grated
3 shallots, finely chopped
salt and black pepper
1 teaspoon thyme
2 bay leaves

Cooking time
20 minutes
Serves 6

Mix the ingredients for the marinade together, beating to combine. Place in a shallow dish with the salmon steaks and leave to marinate for 2 hours.

Drain the salmon and grill, over medium coals, for 15-20 minutes, basting with the marinade and turning from time to time. Serve hot with any remaining marinade.

Opposite: Skewered plaice (see recipe above)
Overleaf: Corn on the grill (see recipe page 75), jacket potatoes
(see recipe page 74), foil-wrapped onions (see recipe page 74)
and steak au poivre (see recipe page 48)

Tuna steaks with mustard

METRIC/IMPERIAL
50 g/2 oz butter, melted
3 teaspoons made mustard
1 tablespoon lemon juice
salt and black pepper
4 individual tuna or cod steaks
Garnish
lemon slices

Cooking time
20 minutes
Serves 4

Illustrated opposite

Combine the melted butter with the mustard, lemon juice and seasoning to taste. Brush half this mixture over the steaks, on both sides, then grill over medium coals for 10 minutes. Turn, brush with the remaining mixture and grill for a further 10 minutes.

Serve hot, with any of the remaining mustard mixture and lemon slices to garnish. Ratatouille (see page 80) would go well with this.

Orange grilled fish

METRIC/IMPERIAL
900 g/2 lb firm white fish
Marinade
4 tablespoons soy sauce
2 tablespoons tomato ketchup
2 tablespoons chopped parsley
150 ml/¼ pint orange juice
grated rind of ½ orange
salt and black pepper

Cooking time
15 minutes
Serves 6

Cut the fish into 2·5-cm/1-inch pieces. Mix the ingredients for the marinade together, beating well. Pour over the fish and leave to marinate for 1 hour.

Drain the fish and thread on six skewers. Grill over hot coals for about 8 minutes, then turn and grill for a further 7 minutes. Baste with the marinade during cooking.

Tuna steaks with mustard (see recipe above)

Grilled fish steaks

METRIC/IMPERIAL
6 individual fish steaks (cod, haddock or halibut)
1 teaspoon salt
¼ teaspoon pepper
50 g/2 oz butter, melted
1 tablespoon lemon juice
1 teaspoon chopped parsley or chives

Sprinkle the fish with the salt and pepper. Mix together the melted butter, lemon juice and parsley or chives. Brush the fish with this mixture. Place the fish steaks on a greased hinged grill and barbecue, over medium coals, for 10–15 minutes, turning once. Baste with the remaining lemon butter towards the end of the cooking time.

Spicy fish kebabs with tropical sauce

Cooking time
10–12 minutes
Serves 4

METRIC/IMPERIAL
675 g/1½ lb firm, chunky white fish
4 cooked jumbo prawns
olive oil to brush
½ teaspoon chilli powder
½ teaspoon paprika pepper
black pepper
Sauce
1 ripe mango
1 tablespoon olive oil
1 teaspoon cornflour
150 ml/¼ pint tropical fruit juice
juice of ½ lime
salt
Garnish
lemon slices

Cut the fish into bite-sized cubes. Peel the prawns and cut the flesh of each into two pieces. Thread the fish and prawns alternately on to eight wooden skewers. Brush lightly with olive oil and sprinkle with the chilli powder, paprika and pepper to taste.

Place on an oiled grill and cook over medium coals for 10–12 minutes, turning frequently. When cooked the fish flesh is firm and the spicy coating is crisp and golden brown.

Meanwhile to prepare the sauce, peel the mango and slice the flesh from the stone. Cut into bite-sized pieces.

Heat the oil in a small pan and add the mango pieces. Cook, stirring over a high heat, for 1 minute. Mix the cornflour with the tropical fruit juice and add to the pan. Bring to the boil, stirring constantly. Allow to simmer for 2–3 minutes. Add the lime juice and salt to taste, blending well.

Serve the kebabs with the sauce and garnished with lemon slices.

Mussel and bacon kebabs

METRIC/IMPERIAL
2·25 litres/4 pints fresh mussels
1 egg, beaten
fine white breadcrumbs
225 g/8 oz streaky bacon, rinds removed
cooking oil
salt and black pepper
lemon wedges

Cooking time
3–5 minutes
Serves 6

Clean the mussels and put them into a large pan with 300 ml/½ pint water. Heat until the shells open. Remove the mussels from their shells, dip in beaten egg and toss in breadcrumbs.

Flatten the bacon rashers with the back of a round-bladed knife until they are very thin. Cut each rasher in half and roll. Place the mussels and bacon rolls alternately on skewers. Brush with the oil and season generously. Cook over hot coals for 3–5 minutes, turning frequently. Serve with lemon wedges and a tartare sauce, if liked.

Spicy skewered shrimps

METRIC/IMPERIAL
450 g/1 lb large shrimps, shelled
lemon slices
Marinade
1 teaspoon chilli powder
1 tablespoon vinegar
1 clove garlic, crushed
salt and black pepper
1 teaspoon chopped parsley
6 tablespoons salad oil

Cooking time
6–10 minutes
Serves 4

Mix the marinade ingredients together, beating to combine well. Marinate the shrimps in this mixture for 2 hours. Remove from the marinade and thread on to four skewers.

Grill over medium coals for 6–10 minutes, turning occasionally and basting with the marinade. Serve hot with slices of lemon.

Sizzling marinated cod

Cooking time
5–8 minutes
Serves 4

METRIC/IMPERIAL
4 cod cutlets
Marinade
4 tablespoons dry white wine or **dry still cider**
1 teaspoon lemon juice
2 teaspoons wholegrain mustard
2 tablespoons olive oil
salt and pepper
Garnish
lemon wedges
chopped parsley

Place the cod cutlets in a shallow dish. Mix the wine or cider with the lemon juice, mustard, oil and seasoning to taste, blending well. Pour over the fish and leave to marinate for at least 1 hour, turning the fish over in the marinade occasionally.

Place on an oiled grill or between an oiled hinged grill rack and cook, over medium coals, for 5–8 minutes, turning once. Baste frequently with the marinade during cooking.

Serve at once with lemon wedges and sprinkled with chopped parsley.

Barbecued lobster

Cooking time
20 minutes
Serves 4

METRIC/IMPERIAL
2 (675-g/1½-lb) lobsters
melted butter
lemon juice
salt and black pepper

To kill a live lobster drive the point of a sharp knife right through the natural cross on the head under which the brain lies, then split in half down the back. Remove the bag in the head and the intestine, a thin grey or black line running down through the tail meat. Crack the large claws with a hammer.

Put the prepared lobster halves on the grill, shell side down, brush with butter and barbecue over hot coals for 15 minutes, basting from time to time with the butter, lemon juice and seasoning. Turn and barbecue for 5 minutes longer. Serve with melted butter and lemon juice.

VEGETABLES

Jacket potatoes

METRIC/IMPERIAL
4 large potatoes
butter

Cooking time
50 minutes
Serves 4
Illustrated on pages 66–67

Scrub the potatoes and dry. Rub with a little butter and
wrap in heavy duty aluminium foil. Place in the centre of the
grill and cook, over medium coals, for about 50 minutes.
Potatoes will be cooked when soft.

To serve, open the foil and cut a cross in the top of each
potato. Fill with butter, soured cream and chives, cottage
cheese or crumbled cooked bacon.

Sizzled potato chips

METRIC/IMPERIAL
450 g/1 lb fresh or frozen potato chips
1 onion, finely chopped
salt and black pepper
50 g/2 oz butter

Cooking time
25–40 minutes
Serves 4

Divide the chips into four equal portions and place each on
a square of aluminium foil. Sprinkle with the chopped
onion and seasoning to taste and dot with the butter.
Fold the foil in to secure packages and cook, over medium
coals, 40 minutes for fresh potato chips or 25 minutes for
frozen, turning from time to time.

Foil-wrapped onions

METRIC/IMPERIAL
4 large onions
25 g/1 oz butter, melted
2 teaspoons Worcestershire sauce
salt and black pepper

Cooking time
45–60 minutes
Serves 4

Illustrated on pages 66–67

Peel and wash the onions and place each one on a square
piece of foil. Brush with the melted butter and
Worcestershire sauce and season to taste. Wrap the foil
halfway up the sides of the onion and cook over medium
coals for 45–60 minutes, turning every 10 minutes.

The onions are cooked when they feel soft to the touch.
Remove the foil and any blackened skin before serving.

Corn on the grill

METRIC/IMPERIAL
4 fresh corn on the cobs (husks intact)
salt and black pepper
Golden glow butter
100 g/4 oz butter
2 tablespoons sieved pimiento
½ teaspoon onion powder (optional)
½ teaspoon paprika pepper

Cooking time
30 minutes
Serves 4

Illustrated on pages 66–67

Remove the large outer husks from the corn, turn back the inner husks and remove silks. Set aside.

Prepare golden glow butter by mixing together the remaining ingredients with a wooden spoon until thoroughly combined. Spread each corn with the softened butter. Pull the husks back over the ears and roast on the grill, over medium to hot coals, for 30 minutes, turning frequently.

Serve hot, with any remaining butter and seasoning to taste.

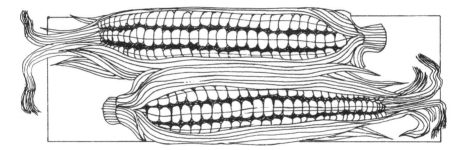

Stuffed grilled mushrooms

METRIC/IMPERIAL
24 large open cap mushrooms
salad oil
2 cloves garlic (optional)
1 medium onion
4 tablespoons chopped parsley
salt and black pepper

Cooking time
20 minutes
Serves 4

Remove the stalks from the mushrooms and set aside. Wipe the caps clean then brush with salad oil and grill, over medium to low coals, for about 15 minutes.

Meanwhile, chop the garlic and onion until fine and mix with the parsley and seasoning to taste. When the mushrooms are almost cooked, put a spoonful of the mixture in the centre of each mushroom cap and cook for a further 5 minutes.

75

Grilled red peppers

METRIC/IMPERIAL
4 large red peppers
1 medium onion
6 tablespoons French dressing (see page 88)

Cooking time
5–10 minutes
Serves 4

Illustrated opposite

Cook the peppers over a hot grill until the skins begin to blacken. Remove from the grill and peel off the skins. Slice into quarters, removing all seeds and pith. Peel and finely chop the onion. Mix the peppers and onion together and place in a small dish. Pour the French dressing over the still warm peppers and marinate for 30 minutes before serving with barbecued beef, chops or sausages.

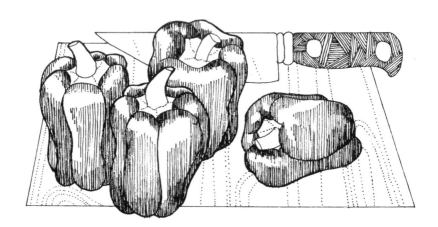

Cheesy-topped tomatoes

METRIC/IMPERIAL
8 medium tomatoes
salad oil
1 medium onion
4 tablespoons finely chopped parsley
75 g/3 oz fresh white breadcrumbs
salt and black pepper
16 small slices cheese

Cooking time
10 minutes
Serves 4

Cut the tomatoes in half and scoop out the seeds. Brush the insides with salad oil. Chop the onion finely and add to the parsley and breadcrumbs. Mix well, season to taste and use to stuff the hollow tomatoes.

Grill, over low coals, for about 5 minutes. Top each half tomato with a slice of cheese and cook for a further 5 minutes. Serve with lamb chops, burgers or sausages.

Grilled red peppers (see recipe above)

Outdoor pilaf

METRIC/IMPERIAL
25 g/1 oz butter
225 g/8 oz long-grain rice
1 small onion, chopped
1 clove garlic, crushed
600–750 ml/1–1¼ pints beef or chicken stock
4 tomatoes, peeled and chopped (optional)
salt and black pepper
50 g/2 oz raisins
2 tablespoons toasted flaked almonds

Cooking time
30 minutes
Serves 4

Illustrated opposite

Heat the butter in a heavy-based frying pan or skillet. Add the rice, onion and garlic and cook, stirring from time to time, until the rice is lightly coloured. Remove from the heat, add the stock, cover and cook for 20 minutes, over medium coals.

Add the tomatoes, if used, and cook for a further 5 minutes, adding a little more stock if the rice seems too dry.

Remove from the heat, season to taste, transfer to a warmed serving dish and sprinkle with the raisins and almonds.

Foiled vegetable medley

METRIC/IMPERIAL
450 g/1 lb courgettes
2 large onions, peeled
4 medium tomatoes, peeled
salt and black pepper
1 clove garlic, chopped
mixed chopped herbs
50 g/2 oz butter

Cooking time
30 minutes
Serves 4

Slice the courgettes and onions thinly and quarter the tomatoes. Mix well together and divide into four equal portions. Place each portion on a square of heavy duty aluminium foil, season to taste, add a little chopped garlic, herbs and butter, and fold the foil to secure the packages.

Cook over medium coals for about 30 minutes, turning once.

Skewered lamb meatballs (see recipe page 52) with outdoor pilaf (see recipe above)

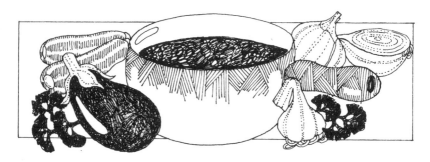

Ratatouille

Cooking time
1 hour
Serves 4-6

METRIC/IMPERIAL
25 g/1 oz butter
3 tablespoons olive oil
2 large onions, thinly sliced
2 cloves garlic, crushed
3 medium aubergines, thinly sliced
1 large green pepper, deseeded and chopped
1 large red pepper, deseeded and chopped
5 medium courgettes, sliced
1 (396-g/14-oz) can tomatoes
1 teaspoon dried basil
1 teaspoon dried rosemary
2 bay leaves
1½ teaspoons salt
¾ teaspoon black pepper
2 tablespoons chopped parsley

Illustrated on page 113

In a large flameproof casserole melt the butter and oil over a moderate heat. Add the onions and garlic and fry, stirring occasionally, for about 5 minutes or until the onions are soft and translucent.

Add the aubergine slices, green and red peppers and courgette slices to the casserole. Fry for 4–5 minutes, shaking the casserole frequently. Add the tomatoes with the can juice, the basil, rosemary, bay leaves and seasoning. Sprinkle over the parsley. Bring to the boil then reduce the heat, cover and simmer for 40–45 minutes until the vegetables are cooked.

Remove from the casserole and serve at once as a vegetable dish, as a basting sauce for meat and poultry or as a starter.

Creamy cabbage

METRIC/IMPERIAL
450 g/1 lb cabbage
6 tablespoons double cream
40 g/1¼ oz butter
salt and black pepper

Cooking time
30 minutes
Serves 4

Shred the cabbage finely and wash well. Line a heavy-based casserole with foil. Place the cabbage in the casserole with the cream, butter and seasoning to taste. Cover with a firm fitting lid and cook over medium to low coals for 30 minutes, or until the cabbage is cooked and creamy.

Variations
Red cabbage may be used instead of white and green cabbage during the late summer and early autumn months. Substitute a combination of single cream and chilli sauce or cheese sauce for a more unusual flavour.

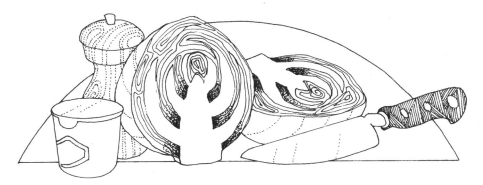

Barbecued baked beans

METRIC/IMPERIAL
100 g/4 oz streaky bacon, rinds removed
25 g/1 oz butter
2 sticks celery
1 medium onion
1 (447-g/15¾-oz) can baked beans
1 tablespoon horseradish sauce
1 teaspoon French mustard

Cooking time
10–12 minutes
Serves 4

Cut the bacon into small pieces and place in a heavy flameproof pan. Heat gently until the fat starts to run. Add the butter and the finely chopped celery and onion. Cook gently, over low coals, until golden.

Add the beans, horseradish sauce and mustard. Cover and heat through over medium coals until the beans are hot. Serve with sausages or hamburgers.

Vegetable kebabs

METRIC/IMPERIAL
6 small potatoes
6 small onions
12 medium mushrooms
2 green peppers
50 g/2 oz butter, melted
½ teaspoon garlic salt
¼ teaspoon black pepper
6 small tomatoes

Peel the potatoes and onions and cook in boiling, salted water until they are barely tender, about 10 minutes. Remove the stems from the mushrooms and wash the caps. Remove the seeds from the peppers and cut into 12 even pieces. Drain the onions and potatoes and alternate on six skewers with the pieces of pepper and mushroom caps. Blend the melted butter, salt and pepper together, and brush the kebabs generously with the mixture. Cook, about 12·5 cm/5 inches above hot coals for 5 minutes. Add a tomato to each skewer, turn the kebabs over and brush with more of the mixture. Continue cooking for about another 5 minutes.

SALADS AND SALAD DRESSINGS

Potato salad

METRIC/IMPERIAL
450 g/1 lb cooked potatoes, peeled and sliced
6 tablespoons mayonnaise
1 tablespoon lemon juice
1 tablespoon olive oil
½ teaspoon salt
½ teaspoon black pepper
2 tablespoons finely chopped chives
4 tablespoons finely chopped leeks

Place three-quarters of the potatoes in a mixing bowl. Pour over the mayonnaise and sprinkle with the lemon juice, oil, salt, pepper and half the chives. Carefully toss until the potatoes are thoroughly coated.

Spoon the mixture into a serving dish. Arrange the remaining potato slices over the top of the salad. Sprinkle with the remaining chives and scatter the leeks around the edge of the dish. Cover and chill for 30 minutes before serving.

Salad mimosa

Serves 4

METRIC/IMPERIAL
2 lettuce hearts, washed and shredded
½ bunch watercress, washed and roughly chopped
2 stalks celery, trimmed and chopped
4½ tablespoons French dressing (see page 88)
2 eggs, hard-boiled and chopped
Garnish
2 oranges, peeled, pith removed and segmented
2 teaspoons olive oil
1 teaspoon white wine vinegar
1 banana, peeled and thinly sliced
1 tablespoon lemon juice
10 green grapes, halved and pipped
1 tablespoon single cream

Combine the lettuce, watercress, celery, French dressing and chopped eggs. Toss until they are all well blended. Transfer to a glass serving dish.

In a small mixing bowl, combine the orange segments, oil and vinegar. In another bowl, combine the banana and lemon juice, and in a third bowl combine the grape halves and cream.

Arrange the fruits and their dressings decoratively over the top of the salad. Serve at once.

Oriental rice salad

METRIC/IMPERIAL
1 small onion, chopped
1 tablespoon oil
2 teaspoons curry powder
1 teaspoon tomato purée
5 tablespoons water
few drops of lemon juice
salt
150 ml/¼ pint mayonnaise
225 g/8 oz long-grain rice, cooked
1 green pepper, deseeded and sliced into rings

Cooking time
10 minutes
Serves 4

Cook the onion in the oil for a few minutes, then add the curry powder and fry for 2–3 minutes. Add the tomato purée, water, lemon juice and salt to taste. Cook for 5 minutes, then strain and cool. Add to the mayonnaise gradually, then mix gently with the hot cooked rice.

Transfer to a warmed serving dish, top with the rings of pepper and serve.

Alternatively, cool the rice and ingredients and serve cold.

Midsummer salad

METRIC/IMPERIAL
2 large slices stale white bread
50 g/2 oz butter
salt
1 clove garlic
1 large Cos lettuce, washed
1 small onion, sliced into thin rings
25 g/1 oz Parmesan cheese
50 g/2 oz button mushrooms, thinly sliced
50 g/2 oz anchovy fillets
6 tablespoons French dressing (see page 88)

Cooking time
5 minutes
Serves 6

Remove the crusts from the bread and cut into 1-cm/½-inch cubes. Fry in the butter until golden brown, drain on absorbent paper and sprinkle with salt.

Rub a large salad bowl with the cut clove of garlic, tear the lettuce into pieces and put into the salad bowl with the remaining salad ingredients. Toss carefully together.

Pour over the French dressing and toss well to coat. Sprinkle with the bread croûtons and serve at once.

Tropical cheese salad

METRIC/IMPERIAL
1 pineapple
175 g/6 oz Cheddar cheese, grated
1 medium dessert apple, cored and sliced
25 g/1 oz walnuts, roughly chopped
25 g/1 oz raisins
4 tablespoons double cream
few drops of Worcestershire sauce
salt and black pepper
few drops of lemon juice
1 tablespoon chopped chives
1 tablespoon chopped parsley
1 lettuce

Cut the pineapple in half lengthways without removing the leafy head. Scoop out the flesh with a sharp knife and cut into bite-sized pieces. Combine the pineapple with the cheese, apple slices, walnuts, raisins, cream, Worcestershire sauce, seasoning to taste, lemon juice, chives and parsley. Pile the mixture back into the pineapple shells. Serve chilled on a bed of lettuce leaves.

Fiesta salad

Cooking time
8 minutes
Serves 6

METRIC/IMPERIAL
2 medium onions, finely sliced
2 medium green peppers, deseeded and coarsely chopped
6 small tomatoes, peeled and chopped
4 rashers streaky bacon, rinds removed
3 tablespoons vinegar
1 teaspoon chilli powder
$\frac{1}{2}$ teaspoon salt
few drops of Tabasco sauce
few drops of Worcestershire sauce
1 lettuce

Separate the onion slices and push into rings. Place in a bowl with the peppers and tomatoes.

Fry the bacon in a frying pan until crisp. Remove and drain on absorbent paper. Pour off the bacon drippings, reserving about 2 tablespoons in the pan. Stir in the vinegar, chilli powder, salt, Tabasco and Worcestershire sauce. Heat to boiling. Pour over the salad vegetables and toss lightly.

Wash and dry the lettuce and use to line a salad bowl. Pile the salad ingredients on top and sprinkle with the crumbled bacon. Serve at once.

Cool cheese salad

Serves 4

METRIC/IMPERIAL
150 ml/¼ pint natural yogurt
2 tablespoons mayonnaise
175 g/6 oz Cheddar cheese, cubed
1 carrot, grated
1 red dessert apple, diced
1 red or green pepper, deseeded and chopped
8 stuffed green olives
50 g/2 oz walnuts, roughly chopped
salt and black pepper
1 tablespoon chopped chives
1 lettuce
Garnish
tomato slices

Mix together the yogurt and the mayonnaise with a wooden spoon until smooth. Add the cheese, carrot, apple, pepper, olives, walnuts, seasoning to taste and chives. Mix well to combine.

Line four individual serving dishes with lettuce leaves. Pile the cheese mixture on top. Chill before serving, garnished with the tomato slices.

Walnut, orange and chicory salad

Serves 4

METRIC/IMPERIAL ·
4 oranges
4 heads chicory, sliced
100 g/4 oz walnuts, chopped
150 ml/¼ pint honey dressing (see page 89)

Peel the oranges, removing as much white pith as possible. Thinly slice into a medium serving dish. Add the chicory and walnuts and pour over the honey dressing. Toss the ingredients together and serve as an accompaniment to barbecued game or poultry.

French dressing

METRIC/IMPERIAL
2 tablespoons red wine vinegar
6 tablespoons olive oil
½ teaspoon salt
¼ teaspoon black pepper
1 clove garlic, crushed (optional)

In a small mixing bowl, beat all the ingredients together with a fork or wire whisk until they are well blended.

Alternatively, put all the ingredients in a screw-topped jar and shake for about 10 seconds. Use as required.

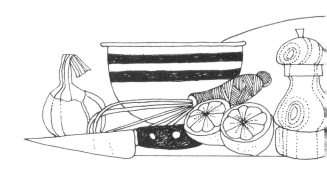

Herb dressing

Makes 300 ml/½ pint

METRIC/IMPERIAL
½ teaspoon chopped chervil
1 teaspoon chopped chives
1 tablespoon chopped parsley
1 teaspoon French mustard
½ teaspoon salt
¼ teaspoon black pepper
1 clove garlic, crushed
225 ml/7½ fl oz olive oil
4 tablespoons tarragon vinegar
2 teaspoons lemon juice

In a small bowl, combine the chervil, chives, parsley, mustard, salt, pepper and garlic with a wooden spoon. Gradually stir in 3 tablespoons of the olive oil. Pour the contents of the bowl into a screw-topped jar. Add the remaining oil, the tarragon vinegar and lemon juice. Firmly screw on the top and shake for 1 minute.

Use as required and store the remainder in the refrigerator until needed.

Honey dressing

Makes 200 ml/7 fl oz

METRIC/IMPERIAL
2 tablespoons clear honey
4 tablespoons lemon juice
6 tablespoons olive oil
$\frac{1}{2}$ teaspoon French mustard
$\frac{1}{4}$ teaspoon salt
$\frac{1}{8}$ teaspoon black pepper

In a small mixing bowl, beat all the ingredients together with a fork or wire whisk, until well blended.

Alternatively, put all the ingredients into a screw-topped jar. Cover the jar and shake for 10 seconds. Use as required.

Onion and paprika dressing

Makes 200 ml/7 fl oz

METRIC/IMPERIAL
6 tablespoons French dressing (see page 88)
1 medium onion, finely chopped
1 tablespoon paprika pepper
$\frac{1}{2}$ teaspoon French mustard
$\frac{1}{2}$ teaspoon sugar
$\frac{1}{2}$ teaspoon black pepper
$4\frac{1}{2}$ tablespoons soured cream

Pour the French dressing into a medium mixing bowl. Add the onion, paprika, mustard, sugar and pepper and beat well with a fork or wire whisk until the ingredients are well blended.

Place the soured cream in another bowl. Gradually add the French dressing mixture to the soured cream, whisking constantly. Serve at once on a mixed salad or pour over freshly cooked vegetables.

Green goddess dressing

METRIC/IMPERIAL
250 ml/8 fl oz mayonnaise
1 teaspoon anchovy essence
3 spring onions, finely chopped
2 tablespoons chopped parsley
2 teaspoons chopped tarragon
1 tablespoon tarragon vinegar
½ teaspoon black pepper
150 ml/¼ pint soured cream

In a medium mixing bowl, combine all the ingredients except the soured cream, and beat well until they are thoroughly blended. Using a metal spoon quickly fold in the soured cream.

Store in the refrigerator and use as required. This dressing makes a delightful addition to mixed salads, or it can be served as a deliciously different filling for jacket potatoes.

Coleslaw dressing

Makes 350 ml/12 fl oz

METRIC/IMPERIAL
300 ml/½ pint mayonnaise
4 tablespoons natural yogurt
1 teaspoon sugar
½ teaspoon salt
1 tablespoon finely grated onion
1 tablespoon finely chopped celery

Blend the mayonnaise with the yogurt, mixing well with a wooden spoon until smooth. Add the remaining dressing ingredients and beat for 1 minute. Use at once.

SAUCES AND MARINADES

A sauce or marinade can make all the difference between an ordinary meal and an unforgettable one. A basting sauce, brushed on the meat as it cooks, adds its own special flavour and keeps the meat juicy and succulent.

A marinade flavours meat and sometimes tenderises it before cooking. Marinate in a tightly covered dish or use a large plastic bag and simply turn the bag to redistribute the marinade. Marinate for several hours in the refrigerator or for at least an hour or two if in a hurry.

Special barbecue sauce

METRIC/IMPERIAL
50 g/2 oz butter
1 onion, finely chopped
1 clove garlic, crushed
2 tablespoons vinegar
150 ml/¼ pint water
1 tablespoon made English mustard
2 tablespoons demerara sugar
1 thick slice lemon
pinch of cayenne pepper
2 tablespoons Worcestershire sauce
6 tablespoons tomato ketchup
2 tablespoons tomato purée
salt and black pepper

Cooking time
25 minutes
Serves 6–8

Melt the butter in a pan and sauté the onion and garlic together gently for about 3 minutes. Stir in the vinegar, water, mustard, sugar, lemon and cayenne. Bring to the boil, cover and simmer for 15 minutes.

Stir in the remaining ingredients, season to taste and continue cooking for a further 5 minutes. Remove the lemon before serving with barbecued meat or poultry.

Orange and lemon barbecue sauce

METRIC/IMPERIAL
2 cloves garlic, crushed
1 large onion, chopped
2–3 tablespoons olive oil
2 teaspoons cornflour
2 tablespoons tomato purée
4 tablespoons demerara sugar
rind and juice of 1 orange
juice of 2 lemons
2 tablespoons Worcestershire sauce
salt and black pepper
150 ml/¼ pint red wine

Cooking time
30 minutes
Serves 6–8

Sauté the garlic and onion in the hot oil until golden in colour. Combine the remaining ingredients well together, then gradually add to the onion, stirring constantly until the sauce thickens. Cover and simmer gently for about 20 minutes. Taste and adjust seasoning if necessary. Strain and serve hot with game, poultry or meat.

Tomato sauce

METRIC/IMPERIAL
4 large ripe tomatoes, peeled, or 1 (227-g/8-oz) can tomatoes
4 tablespoons tomato ketchup
1 tablespoon red wine vinegar
2 tablespoons olive oil
few drops of Tabasco sauce
pinch of dry mustard
salt and black pepper

Chop the tomatoes coarsely and mix with the remaining ingredients. Season to taste and serve with barbecued sausages, chops or chicken drumsticks.

Cucumber and yogurt sauce

Serves 4

METRIC/IMPERIAL
300 ml/½ pint natural yogurt
½ large cucumber
salt and black pepper
few drops of Tabasco sauce

Beat the yogurt with a wooden spoon until quite smooth. Peel the cucumber and cut into small dice. Stir into the yogurt. Season to taste with salt, pepper and Tabasco.

Chill before serving with barbecued lamb or chicken.

Creamy bacon sauce

Serves 4

METRIC/IMPERIAL
2 rashers rindless streaky bacon, chopped
6 tablespoons mayonnaise
2 tablespoons mild prepared mustard
salt and pepper
1 tablespoon chopped chives or finely chopped spring
** onion**

Place the bacon in a small pan and dry fry until golden and crisp. Drain and leave until cold.

Mix the bacon with the mayonnaise, mustard, seasoning to taste and the chives or spring onion, blending well.

Chill lightly before serving with burgers, barbecued lamb, chicken and jacket potatoes.

Gooseberry herb sauce

METRIC/IMPERIAL
225 g/8 oz gooseberries, topped and tailed
4½ tablespoons water
2 tablespoons castor sugar
25 g/1 oz butter
1 tablespoon chopped fennel
1 tablespoon chopped parsley

Cooking time
12 minutes
Serves 4

Illustrated on page 37

Place the gooseberries in a small pan with the water, sugar, butter and most of the fennel and parsley. Bring to the boil, reduce the heat and simmer for about 10 minutes.

Remove from the heat, pour into a warmed heatproof dish and sprinkle with the remaining fennel and parsley.

Serve with barbecued mackerel.

Lemon sauce

METRIC/IMPERIAL
2 shallots, finely chopped
50 g/2 oz butter
1 tablespoon flour
300 ml/½ pint dry white wine or cider
salt and black pepper
juice of 1 large lemon
1 lemon, finely sliced
1 tablespoon finely chopped parsley

Cooking time
15 minutes
Makes 300 ml/½ pint

Cook the shallots in the butter until softened but not browned. Add the flour and cook for 1 minute, stirring well. Take off the heat and gradually add the wine or cider, stirring until smooth. Bring to the boil and simmer gently for 5 minutes. Season to taste with the salt and pepper, add the lemon juice and sliced lemon and finally the chopped parsley.

Serve hot with barbecued fish or chicken.

Onion burgers (see recipe page 49) and bacon-wrapped
sausages (see recipe page 57)

Mustard sauce

Cooking time
5-6 minutes
Makes 450 ml/¾ pint

METRIC/IMPERIAL
40 g/1½ oz butter
25 g/1 oz flour
450 ml/¾ pint milk
salt and pepper
1 tablespoon dry mustard
1 tablespoon wine vinegar
1 teaspoon castor sugar

Melt 25 g/1 oz of the butter in a pan, stir in the flour and cook for 1 minute. Gradually add the milk, beating well until the sauce is smooth. Bring to the boil and simmer for 2–3 minutes. Season to taste.

Blend the mustard powder with the vinegar and stir into the sauce. Add the sugar. Check seasoning and stir in the remaining butter.

Serve mustard sauce with barbecued beef, mackerel, sausages and steaks.

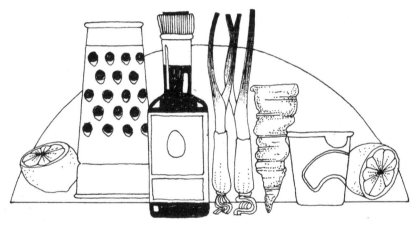

Cidered apple sauce

METRIC/IMPERIAL   Makes about 300 ml/½ pint
2 Granny Smith apples
3 tablespoons cider and honey marinade (see page 99)
150 ml/¼ pint soured cream

Peel, core and process the apples in a blender or food processor until almost smooth.

Add the cider and honey marinade and soured cream. Mix well to blend.

Chill lightly before serving as a cold sauce for duck, chicken and barbecued fish.

Skewered rabbit with mustard (see recipe page 60)   **97**

Spiced orange basting and serving sauce

METRIC/IMPERIAL   Makes about 450 ml/$\frac{3}{4}$ pint
6 tablespoons light soft brown sugar
4 tablespoons soy sauce
150 ml/$\frac{1}{4}$ pint orange juice
150 ml/$\frac{1}{4}$ pint dry white wine
4 tablespoons water
$\frac{1}{2}$ teaspoon paprika pepper
$\frac{1}{2}$ teaspoon dry mustard
pinch of ground cinnamon
2–3 drops of Tabasco sauce
2 teaspoons cornflour

Mix the sugar with the soy sauce, orange juice, wine, water, paprika, mustard, cinnamon and Tabasco, blending well. Bring to the boil, reduce the heat and simmer for 5 minutes.

Use to baste chicken, duck, turkey or pork during barbecue cooking.

Thicken any remaining sauce by blending the cornflour with a little water. Stir into the sauce mixture, blending well. Bring to boil, stirring constantly, until smooth and thickened. Serve hot as a pouring sauce.

Redcurrant and mustard sauce

METRIC/IMPERIAL   Makes about 150 ml/$\frac{1}{4}$ pint
4 tablespoons redcurrant sauce
2 tablespoons mild prepared mustard
1 tablespoon lemon juice

Place the redcurrant sauce, mustard and lemon juice in a small pan. Heat gently, stirring constantly, until smooth and blended.

Serve warm or cold with barbecued chicken, burgers, fatty meats like duck, game and pork or frankfurters.

Chilli marinade

Makes 300 ml/½ pint

METRIC/IMPERIAL
1 teaspoon chilli powder
1 teaspoon celery salt
2 tablespoons soft brown sugar
2 tablespoons wine or tarragon vinegar
2 tablespoons Worcestershire sauce
3 tablespoons tomato ketchup
150 ml/¼ pint beef stock or water
few drops of Tabasco sauce

Combine all the ingredients together with a fork or wire whisk to thoroughly blend. Pour over the food and leave in the refrigerator, turning from time to time, until required.

Use this marinade for poultry, steaks, spareribs, chops and roasts.

Cider and honey marinade

Makes about 250 ml/8 fl oz

METRIC/IMPERIAL
2 tablespoons soy sauce
3 tablespoons cider vinegar
1 tablespoon clear honey
1 tablespoon safflower oil
150 ml/¼ pint dry still cider

Beat the soy sauce with the vinegar, honey, oil and cider to thoroughly blend. Pour over the chosen food and leave to marinate in the refrigerator for 2–4 hours. Turn the food occasionally to coat thoroughly.

Use as a marinade and basting sauce for steaks, duck, chicken and spareribs.

Chive mustard marinade

METRIC/IMPERIAL
4 tablespoons salad oil
3 tablespoons lemon juice
2 tablespoons chive mustard
1 teaspoon salt
½ teaspoon freshly ground black pepper

Beat the oil with the lemon juice, chive mustard, salt and pepper to blend well. Pour over the chosen food and leave to marinate in the refrigerator for at least 3 hours. Turn the food occasionally to coat thoroughly.

Use as a marinade and basting sauce for steaks, lamb, chicken and fish.

Sage and onion yogurt marinade

Makes about 200 ml/7 fl oz

METRIC/IMPERIAL
150 ml/¼ pint natural yogurt
2 tablespoons sage and onion mustard
1 tablespoon brown sugar
salt and pepper

Mix the yogurt with the sage and onion mustard, sugar and seasoning to taste, blending well. Pour over the chosen food and leave to marinate for at least 3 hours. Turn the food occasionally to coat thoroughly.

Use as a marinade and basting sauce for pork and chicken.

RELISHES AND CHUTNEYS

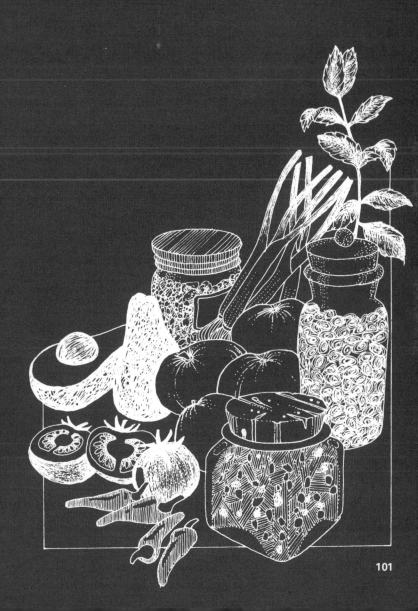

Pepper relish

Cooking time
35–50 minutes
Makes 1·25 kg/2½ lb

METRIC/IMPERIAL
6 medium red peppers
8 red or green chillies
450 g/1 lb tomatoes
225 g/8 oz onions
225 g/8 oz cooking apples
2 teaspoons salt
450 ml/¾ pint brown malt vinegar
225 g/8 oz granulated sugar

Remove the core and seeds from the peppers and chillies. Cut the peppers into quarters. Peel the tomatoes and peel and quarter the onions and the cooking apples.

Coarsely mince the ingredients together. Place in a heavy-based pan with the remaining ingredients. Bring to the boil, reduce the heat and simmer until thick, about 30–45 minutes. Cool, pot and cover.

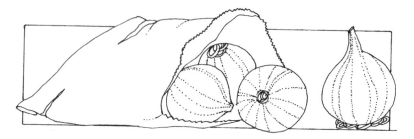

Corn relish

Cooking time
25–35 minutes
Makes 900 g/2 lb

METRIC/IMPERIAL
1 red pepper
1 medium onion
100 g/4 oz celery
450 g/1 lb fresh, canned or thawed frozen sweetcorn
225 g/8 oz granulated sugar
600 ml/1 pint white malt vinegar
2 teaspoons salt
2 teaspoons dry mustard

Remove the core and seeds from the pepper and cut into quarters. Peel and quarter the onion. Pass the pepper, onion, celery and three-quarters of the sweetcorn through a mincer. Place in a heavy-based saucepan with the remaining sweetcorn and ingredients. Bring to the boil, reduce the heat and simmer for 20–30 minutes, until thick. Cool, pot and cover.

Cucumber relish

Cooking time
20–30 minutes
Makes 2 kg/4½ lb

METRIC/IMPERIAL
2 large cucumbers
1 head celery
1 large red pepper
1 large green pepper
450 g/1 lb onions
2 spring onions
900 ml/1½ pints white malt vinegar
1 teaspoon curry powder
1 teaspoon dry mustard
½ teaspoon cayenne pepper
½ teaspoon paprika pepper
½ teaspoon ground ginger
450 g/1 lb granulated sugar

Illustrated on page 37

Wash the cucumbers and cut into short lengths. Scrub the celery and trim. Discard the core and seeds from the peppers and cut into quarters. Peel and quarter the onions. Chop the spring onions. Pass all the prepared ingredients through a mincer.

Put the vinegar in a heavy-based saucepan with the spices. Bring to the boil. Add the minced ingredients and sugar and bring back to the boil. Simmer for 20–30 minutes until thick. Cool, pot and cover.

Mint relish

Cooking time
20–30 minutes
Makes 2·25 kg/5 lb

METRIC/IMPERIAL
900 g/2 lb cooking apples
450 g/1 lb onions
225 g/8 oz tomatoes
225 g/8 oz small sprigs of mint
100 g/4 oz seedless raisins
1 teaspoon dry mustard
2 teaspoons salt
½ teaspoon cayenne pepper
600 ml/1 pint brown malt vinegar
225 g/8 oz soft brown sugar

Peel, core and chop the apples roughly. Peel and chop the onions. Peel, deseed and roughly chop the tomatoes. Chop the mint leaves and raisins finely.

Place all the ingredients in a heavy-based saucepan. Bring to the boil, stirring, then simmer, uncovered, until the mixture has a thick consistency, about 20–30 minutes. Cool, pot and cover.

Avocado relish

METRIC/IMPERIAL
2 avocados
juice of ½ lemon
225 g/8 oz tomatoes
1 bunch spring onions
black pepper
Dressing
2 tablespoons oil
½ tablespoon lime juice
½ tablespoon lemon juice

Peel the avocados and cut the flesh into small dice. Sprinkle with the lemon juice. Peel and chop the tomatoes, discarding seeds and juice, and add to the avocado. Trim and finely chop the spring onions. Mix with the avocado and tomato mixture. Add black pepper to taste.

Make the dressing by combining the oil, lime and lemon juice together. Pour over the avocado and tomato mixture. Chill before serving as an accompaniment to any chicken or dry fish dish.

Instant chutney

Cooking time
8 minutes
Makes 450 g/1 lb

METRIC/IMPERIAL
1 dessert apple
1 medium onion
3 medium tomatoes
2 stalks celery
1 red pepper
1 tablespoon chopped mint
1 tablespoon horseradish sauce
1 clove garlic, minced
25 g/1 oz sugar
2 tablespoons vinegar
1 teaspoon salt
black pepper

Peel, core and finely grate the apple and onion. Peel the tomatoes and roughly chop. Scrub and finely chop the celery. Core and deseed the pepper and cut into small dice. Place with the remaining ingredients in a medium saucepan and bring to the boil. Reduce the heat, cover and simmer for 5 minutes.

Serve hot or cold with barbecued steak, chops, kebabs, sausages and spareribs.

SAVOURY BUTTERS

Garlic butter

METRIC/IMPERIAL
2 cloves garlic
50 g/2 oz butter, softened
$\frac{1}{4}$ teaspoon freshly ground black pepper

Peel the cloves of garlic and place in a small pan with a little water. Bring to the boil, reduce the heat and simmer for 5 minutes. Drain thoroughly.

Finely chop the garlic and place in a bowl. Add the butter and pepper and beat until smooth and blended. Cover and chill until required.

Use for making garlic French bread, on steaks, lamb chops or seafood.

Mustard butter

METRIC/IMPERIAL
50 g/2 oz butter
2 teaspoons wholegrain mustard
salt and pepper

Place the butter in a bowl and cream until soft. Add the mustard and seasoning to taste. Beat until smooth and blended. Cover and chill until required.

Use on beef, lamb, ham, gammon, shellfish or barbecued oily fish like mackerel.

Chive butter

METRIC/IMPERIAL
50 g/2 oz butter
2 teaspoons finely chopped chives
1 teaspoon lemon juice
salt and pepper

Place the butter in a bowl and cream until soft. Add the chives, lemon juice and seasoning to taste. Beat until smooth and blended. Cover and chill until required.

Use on seafood, chicken, lamb and barbecued fish.

Horseradish butter

METRIC/IMPERIAL
50 g/2 oz butter
2 teaspoons finely grated horseradish
salt and pepper

Place the butter in a bowl and cream until soft. Add the horseradish and seasoning to taste. Beat until smooth and blended. Cover and chill until required.

Use on beef or barbecued fish.

Green butter

METRIC/IMPERIAL
2 sprigs tarragon
2 sprigs chervil
2 sprigs parsley
2 small spinach leaves
50 g/2 oz butter
1 teaspoon finely grated onion
salt and pepper

Place the tarragon, chervil, parsley and spinach in a bowl. Cover with boiling water and leave to stand for 5 minutes. Drain and rinse in cold water then dry on absorbent kitchen paper. Chop finely.

Place the butter in a bowl and cream until soft. Add the chopped herbs, onion and seasoning to taste. Beat until smooth and blended. Cover and chill until required.

Use on fish, shellfish, lamb and poultry.

Devilled butter

METRIC/IMPERIAL
50 g/2 oz butter
½ teaspoon dry mustard powder
1 teaspoon Worcestershire sauce
1 teaspoon lemon juice
salt and cayenne pepper

Place the butter in a bowl and cream until soft. Add the mustard, Worcestershire sauce, lemon juice and salt and cayenne to taste. Beat until smooth and blended. Cover and chill until required.

Use on shellfish, ham, gammon and pork.

Cinnamon butter

METRIC/IMPERIAL
50 g/2 oz unsalted butter
25 g/1 oz soft brown sugar
½ teaspoon ground cinnamon
2 teaspoons dark rum (optional)

Place the butter in a bowl and cream until soft. Add the sugar, cinnamon and rum if used. Beat until smooth and blended. Cover and chill until required.

Use on fruits like apples, pears, oranges, pineapple and peaches.

Brandy or rum butter

METRIC/IMPERIAL
50 g/2 oz unsalted butter
50 g/2 oz castor sugar
¼ teaspoon finely grated lemon or orange rind
1½ teaspoons boiling water
½ teaspoon lemon or orange juice
2 tablespoons brandy or rum

Place the butter in a bowl and cream until soft. Add the sugar and lemon or orange rind and beat until creamy. Add the boiling water and continue to beat until the sugar has dissolved.

Add the lemon or orange juice and brandy or rum. Beat well to blend. Cover and chill until required.

Use on fruits like bananas, oranges, mangoes and guavas.

ACCOMPANIMENTS

Hot garlic bread

METRIC/IMPERIAL
1 French loaf
100 g/4 oz butter
3 cloves garlic, finely minced
1½ tablespoons finely minced parsley

Cooking time
10 minutes
Serves 6

Thickly slice the French loaf crossways almost to its base along its length.

Cream the butter with the garlic and parsley until thoroughly blended. Spread each segment with a lavish helping of the butter. Wrap the loaf in foil, dull side out, and barbecue over medium coals for about 10 minutes, turning once. Remove from the grill, unwrap, pull the slices apart to free and serve hot.

Potato and tomato pan fry

METRIC/IMPERIAL
15 g/½ oz butter
1 tablespoon oil
3 potatoes, par-boiled and diced
3 tomatoes, peeled and chopped
100 g/4 oz frozen peas
salt and pepper

Cooking time
15–20 minutes
Serves 2–4

Heat the butter and oil in a frying pan over hot coals. Add the potato and cook for 5 minutes, stirring occasionally, until golden.

Add the tomatoes, peas and seasoning to taste, blending well. Cover and cook for 10 minutes, stirring occasionally.

Serve hot as an accompaniment to barbecued meat and fish.

Herb spread

Makes 150 g/5 oz

METRIC/IMPERIAL
100 g/4 oz cream cheese
1 tablespoon mayonnaise
1 teaspoon finely chopped parsley
1 teaspoon finely chopped chives
1 teaspoon finely chopped sorrel leaves
¼ teaspoon salt
⅛ teaspoon white pepper

Combine all the ingredients together in a medium mixing bowl, beating with a wooden spoon until well blended. Place the bowl in the refrigerator and chill for 30 minutes before serving.

Mint and chive spread

METRIC/IMPERIAL
50 g/2 oz unsalted butter
1 tablespoon finely chopped mint
1 tablespoon finely chopped chives
½ teaspoon lemon juice

Combine all the ingredients in a medium mixing bowl, beating with a wooden spoon until well blended. Place the bowl in the refrigerator and chill for 30 minutes before serving.

Hot and cold spread

Makes 150 g/5 oz

METRIC/IMPERIAL
100 g/4 oz mild cream cheese
1 tablespoon mayonnaise
1 tablespoon finely chopped radishes
1 tablespoon finely chopped watercress

Combine all the ingredients in a medium mixing bowl, beating with a wooden spoon until well blended. Place in the refrigerator and chill for 30 minutes before serving.

Quick barbecue bean hotpot

METRIC/IMPERIAL
Cooking time
10–15 minutes
Serves 6–8

8 pork sausages
4 tablespoons oil
1 large onion, finely sliced
2 green or red peppers, cored, deseeded and sliced
generous pinch paprika pepper
salt and pepper
1 clove garlic, crushed
2 (450-g/1-lb) cans barbecue beans

Brush the sausages lightly with oil. Cook, over hot coals, for about 4–5 minutes each side.

Meanwhile, heat 3 tablespoons oil in a frying pan on the barbecue (alternatively cook in the kitchen on the hob if liked). Add the onion and sauté for 3–4 minutes. Add the peppers, paprika, seasoning to taste and the garlic, blending well. Cook over moderate heat for a further 3 minutes.

Add the beans, blending well. Cook for 2-4 minutes until hot. Spoon into a flameproof casserole with the barbecued sausages. Cover the casserole and keep warm on the edge of the barbecue. Serve hot as a hearty main course accompaniment.

Bacon and apple stir fry

METRIC/IMPERIAL
50 g/2 oz butter
1 tablespoon oil
4 unsmoked gammon *or* **bacon steaks, cut into**
  5-cm/2-inch strips
2 onions, thickly sliced
3 dessert apples, cored and sliced
4 tablespoons dry cider
pepper
1 tablespoon chopped parsley

Cooking time
about 15 minutes
Serves 6-8

Place the butter and oil in a frying pan. Heat over moderate coals until hot and bubbly. Add the gammon or bacon, onion and apple. Fry quickly, turning frequently, until the gammon or bacon is cooked and golden.

Add the cider and allow to simmer for 2-4 minutes. Season with pepper to taste and sprinkle with parsley.

Serve hot as a main course accompaniment.

Soured cream topping for jacket baked potatoes

METRIC/IMPERIAL   Serves 4–6
300 ml/½ pint soured cream
2 tablespoons lemon juice
pinch of salt
¼ teaspoon paprika pepper
1 tablespoon molasses sugar
1 teaspoon finely chopped chives

Mix the soured cream with the lemon juice, salt, paprika, sugar and chives, blending well.

Serve lightly chilled on baked and split open jacket potatoes.

Grilled marinated sardines (see recipe page 62) and ratatouille
(see recipe page 80)
Overleaf: Foil-wrapped pork chops and grilled mushrooms

DESSERTS

Crunchy baked apples with chocolate sauce

METRIC/IMPERIAL
4 medium cooking apples
75 g/3 oz muesli
2 tablespoons golden syrup
juice of 1 lemon
25 g/1 oz butter
Sauce
175 g/6 oz plain chocolate
150 ml/¼ pint mandarin orange juice
2 tablespoons golden syrup

Cooking time
45–60 minutes
Serves 4

Core the apples and make a shallow cut through the skin around the middle of each. Place each apple on a large double-thickness piece of heavy-duty aluminium foil.

Mix the muesli with the golden syrup and lemon juice, blending well. Use to fill the apple cavities, pressing down well. Dot with the butter then wrap up each apple to enclose totally. Place directly on the grill and cook over medium coals for 45–60 minutes, turning occasionally.

Meanwhile, prepare the sauce. Place the chocolate, broken into pieces, and 3 tablespoons of the mandarin juice in a small saucepan and heat gently until melted. Add the golden syrup and the remaining juice. Bring to the boil, stirring constantly. Allow to simmer, uncovered, for 10 minutes, stirring occasionally. Leave the sauce to cool slightly.

Serve the apples hot with the warm sauce poured over.

Baked pears with lemon cream

METRIC/IMPERIAL
4 medium dessert pears
4 teaspoons brown sugar
40 g/1½ oz butter
Lemon cream
50 g/2 oz castor sugar
½ teaspoon grated lemon rind
1 tablespoon cornflour
250 ml/8 fl oz single cream
2 egg yolks, beaten with ½ teaspoon vanilla essence

Cooking time
20–30 minutes
Serves 4

Halve and core the pears. Place each serving, i.e. 2 pear halves, on a large double-thickness piece of heavy-duty aluminium foil. Scatter each portion with the brown sugar and dot with the butter. Wrap up each serving to enclose completely.

Place directly on the grill and cook over medium coals for 20–30 minutes, turning occasionally.

Meanwhile to make the lemon cream, blend the castor sugar with the lemon rind and cornflour in a small pan. Gradually add the cream, blending well. Cook over a gentle heat, stirring constantly until thickened. Blend a small amount of the thickened sauce with the egg yolk mixture then return to the pan, blending well. Cook over a gentle heat for 2–3 minutes. Remove from the heat and allow to cool slightly until the pears are cooked.

Serve the hot baked pears with the warm lemon cream.

Golden fruit slices

METRIC/IMPERIAL
450 g/1 lb sliced fresh fruit (apricots, plums, peaches or cherries, for example)
25 g/1 oz butter
2 tablespoons orange juice
2 tablespoons Grand Marnier *or* **Cointreau liqueur**
2 tablespoons demerara sugar (optional)

Cooking time
5–10 minutes
Serves 4

Place the fruit on a large double-thickness piece of heavy-duty aluminium foil. Dot with the butter and spoon over the orange juice and liqueur. Sprinkle with the sugar if used.

Turn up the edges of the foil to partially enclose the fruit. Place on the grill and cook over hot coals for 5–10 minutes.

Serve hot or warm with ice cream.

Fresh lime mousse

METRIC/IMPERIAL
3 eggs, separated
100 g/4 oz castor sugar
finely grated rind and juice of 2 limes
3 teaspoons powdered gelatine
6 tablespoons double cream
Decoration
whipped cream
lime slices

Serves 6

Place the egg yolks in a deep bowl with the castor sugar and grated rind of the limes. Whisk until thick and mousse-like.

Meanwhile, soften the gelatine in a small bowl in the lime juice. Dissolve by standing the bowl in a pan of gently simmering water.

Whip the cream until lightly thick and fold through the mousse with the dissolved gelatine. Lastly fold in the stiffly beaten egg whites and turn into six individual dishes. Refrigerate until firm then decorate with swirls of whipped cream and twists of lime.

Tipsy trifle

METRIC/IMPERIAL
6 trifle sponge cakes, each sliced into 2 layers
3 tablespoons orange-flavoured liqueur
2 tablespoons fresh orange juice
275 g/10 oz sugar
300 ml/½ pint custard
4 large oranges, peeled, pith removed and thinly sliced
150 ml/¼ pint double cream, whipped

Place the sponge slices in one layer in a large dish. Sprinkle over the liqueur and orange juice and set aside for 30 minutes, until all the liquid has been absorbed.

In a heavy-based saucepan, dissolve the sugar over a low heat, shaking the pan occasionally. Increase the heat to moderate and boil the syrup, shaking the pan occasionally, until it turns a rich golden brown. Remove from the heat and place the saucepan in a bowl of hot water to keep the caramel warm.

Arrange one-third of the soaked orange sponge slices in a medium glass serving dish. Spoon over one-third of the custard, smoothing it evenly with the back of the spoon. Lay one-third of the orange slices over the custard to cover it completely. Trickle over one-third of the caramel in a thin stream.

Continue making layers in the same way, ending with a layer of caramel-coated orange slices. Place the trifle in the refrigerator and chill for 2 hours.

Fill a piping bag, fitted with a star-shaped nozzle, with the whipped cream. Remove the trifle from the refrigerator and pipe the cream over the top in decorative swirls. Serve chilled.

South Sea banana bubbles

METRIC/IMPERIAL
4 firm bananas, thickly sliced
50 g/2 oz butter
2 tablespoons orange syrup
2 tablespoons dark rum
1 orange, peeled and sliced

Cut four pieces of heavy-duty aluminium foil, each large enough to comfortably enclose a whole sliced banana. Place one sliced banana in the centre of each. Dot with the butter, spoon over the syrup and rum and cover with the orange slices. Seal the edges of the foil to make parcels.

Place on the grill and cook, over medium to hot coals, for about 10 minutes.

Serve hot with pouring cream if liked.

Mocha mousse

METRIC/IMPERIAL
100 g/4 oz plain cooking chocolate
4 tablespoons strong black coffee
4 eggs, separated
150 g/5 oz light brown sugar
Decoration
whipped cream
grated chocolate curls

In a small heavy-based saucepan melt the chocolate in the coffee over a low heat. As soon as the chocolate has melted, remove the pan from the heat and set aside to cool for 10 minutes.

In a large mixing bowl, beat the egg yolks and sugar together with a wire whisk until the mixture is pale and thick. Beat in the cooled chocolate and coffee mixture.

In a medium mixing bowl, whisk the egg whites until very stiff. With a metal spoon fold the egg whites into the chocolate mixture until completely blended. Spoon the mousse into four individual serving dishes. Chill and allow to set before decorating with swirls of whipped cream and chocolate curls.

Fruit kebabs with honey-lemon sauce

Cooking time
5 minutes

METRIC/IMPERIAL
Choose from:
peach halves
pear halves
apple chunks
red and green maraschino cherries
pineapple cubes
stuffed dates
orange slices
Sauce
100 g/4 oz honey
1½ tablespoons lemon juice

The easiest of desserts; prepare a selection of fresh and canned fruits and leave guests to assemble their own choice of fruits and grill to their liking.

Cut a variety of the above fruits into uniform pieces. Thread the fruit on to long skewers.

Prepare the sauce by blending together the honey and lemon. Liberally brush over the fruit kebabs. Grill over medium coals until hot, about 5 minutes. Serve hot with any remaining sauce.

Raspberry pavlova

Cooking time
1 hour
Serves 6

METRIC/IMPERIAL
3 egg whites
175 g/6 oz castor sugar
½ teaspoon vanilla essence
½ teaspoon vinegar
2 teaspoons cornflour
300 ml/½ pint double cream, whipped
450 g/1 lb fresh or frozen raspberries

Whisk the egg whites until stiff. Gradually add the sugar, whisking until the mixture is thick and glossy. Whisk in the vanilla, vinegar and cornflour.

Mark out a 20-cm/8-inch circle on a piece of non-stick baking paper. Place on a baking tray. Spoon the mixture within this circle, building it up around the edges. Bake in a cool oven (140°C, 275°F, Gas Mark 1) for 50–60 minutes, until the meringue is crisp on the outside. Cool and carefully remove the paper.

Fill the centre of the pavlova with two-thirds of the whipped cream. Place the remaining cream in a piping bag fitted with a star-shaped nozzle. Pipe swirls of cream around the edge of the pavlova and decorate with the raspberries. Any remaining raspberries may be piled in the centre of the pavlova.

Honeydew melon with blackcurrant iced mousse

Cooking time
5 minutes
Serves 6

METRIC/IMPERIAL
300 ml/½ pint blackcurrant juice
150 ml/¼ pint water
50 g/2 oz sugar
grated rind and juice of 1 lemon
15 g/½ oz powdered gelatine, dissolved in 2 tablespoons hot water
1 egg white
1 large honeydew melon

Turn the thermostat of the refrigerator to its coldest setting.

In a saucepan, combine the blackcurrant juice, water, sugar and lemon rind. Bring to the boil over a moderately high heat and boil for 4 minutes. Remove the pan from the heat and stir in the lemon juice and dissolved gelatine. Pour the mixture through a strainer into an ice-cube or freezer tray. Place in the ice-making compartment of the refrigerator and chill for 30 minutes.

In a small bowl, whisk the egg white until stiff. Whisk the

chilled blackcurrant mixture into the egg white. Spoon back into the ice-cube tray and freeze for a further hour.

Remove from the refrigerator and turn into a mixing bowl. Whisk for 1 minute. Return to the ice-making compartment and freeze for 4 hours.

With a sharp knife, slice the melon crossways into six slices. Scoop out the seeds and place the slices on individual plates. Spoon the mousse into the centre of each piece. Serve at once.

Meringues Chantilly

METRIC/IMPERIAL
Meringues
4 egg whites
225 g/8 oz plus 1 teaspoon castor sugar
Crème Chantilly
300 ml/½ pint double cream
2 teaspoons castor sugar
½ teaspoon vanilla essence

Cooking time
1½ hours
Serves 6

Preheat the oven to cool (140°C, 275°F, Gas Mark 1). Line two baking trays with non-stick silicone paper and set aside.

In a large mixing bowl, whisk the egg whites until they form stiff peaks. Add four teaspoons of the sugar and continue whisking for 1 minute. With a metal spoon, quickly and carefully fold all but 1 teaspoon of the sugar into the egg whites.

Spoon or pipe the mixture into twelve mounds or swirls on the baking trays. Sprinkle with the remaining sugar. Place in the oven and bake the meringues for 1 hour, changing the trays around halfway through baking, or until firm and lightly beige in colour.

Remove the baking trays from the oven and carefully turn the meringues over. Gently press the centres to make a shallow indentation in each meringue. Return to the oven and bake for a further 30 minutes.

Remove the baking trays from the oven and allow the meringues to cool completely.

In a medium mixing bowl, beat the cream with a wire whisk until it is very thick. Add the sugar and the vanilla essence and continue beating until the cream is stiff.

Sandwich pairs of meringues with the flavoured cream and serve.

Redcurrant cheesecake

METRIC/IMPERIAL

Serves 6–8

100 g/4 oz plus 1 teaspoon butter, melted
225 g/8 oz digestive biscuits, crushed
1 teaspoon ground cinnamon
450 g/1 lb cream cheese
50 g/2 oz castor sugar
6 tablespoons single cream
575 g/1¼ lb redcurrants, topped and tailed
15 g/½ oz powdered gelatine, dissolved in 2 tablespoons hot water
300 ml/½ pint double cream
1 egg white, stiffly whisked

Lightly grease a 23-cm/9-inch loose-bottomed cake tin with the teaspoon of butter.

In a medium mixing bowl, combine the crushed biscuits, the remaining melted butter and the cinnamon with a wooden spoon. Line the base of the tin with this mixture, pressing it firmly against the bottom. Set aside.

In a medium mixing bowl, beat the cream cheese and sugar together with a wooden spoon until smooth and creamy. Stir in the single cream and 450 g/1 lb redcurrants. Beat in the dissolved gelatine mixture and spoon the mixture on to the biscuit crust. Place in the refrigerator to chill for 30 minutes, or until set.

Meanwhile, in a large mixing bowl, beat the double cream with a wire whisk until it forms stiff peaks. With a large metal spoon, fold the egg white into this mixture.

Remove the cheesecake from the refrigerator. Spoon the cream mixture on the cheesecake, making swirling patterns with the back of the spoon.

Sprinkle the remaining redcurrants over the cream. Chill and serve.

HOT AND COLD DRINKS

Brandied coffee cream

Cooking time
3–4 minutes
Serves 8

METRIC/IMPERIAL
100 g/4 oz sugar
5 eggs
3 tablespoons brandy
300 ml/½ pint milk
300 ml/½ pint single cream
600 ml/1 pint strong black coffee
3 tablespoons double cream, stiffly whipped
25 g/1 oz plain or milk chocolate, grated

In a large mixing bowl, beat the sugar and eggs together with a fork or wire whisk until well blended. Set aside.

In a large saucepan, heat the brandy, milk, single cream and coffee together over a moderate heat until hot but not boiling. Remove the pan from the heat and gradually pour into the egg and sugar mixture, whisking constantly until the ingredients are well blended.

Pour the brandied coffee into eight heatproof glasses. Top with a little whipped cream and grated chocolate and serve immediately.

Mulled claret

Cooking time
5 minutes
Makes 1·75 litres/3 pints

METRIC/IMPERIAL
1·4 litres/2½ pints dry red Bordeaux wine
1 tablespoon finely grated orange rind
1 tablespoon finely grated lemon rind
225 g/8 oz sugar
½ teaspoon ground cloves
½ teaspoon grated nutmeg
300 ml/½ pint brandy

Put the wine, orange and lemon rinds, sugar, cloves and nutmeg into a stainless steel or enamel saucepan. Place over a moderate heat and bring to the boil, stirring constantly to dissolve the sugar. Remove from the heat and pour the wine mixture into a large punch bowl. Set aside.

In a small saucepan, warm the brandy over a low heat until hot but not boiling. Remove from the heat and pour into the punch bowl. Ignite the punch if liked. When the flames die down, serve the punch in heatproof glasses.

Golden fruit punch

METRIC/IMPERIAL
15 ice cubes
300 ml/½ pint white grape juice
300 ml/½ pint apple juice
600 ml/1 pint pineapple juice
475 ml/16 fl oz dry ginger ale
1 small pineapple, peeled and finely chopped *or*
1 (339-g/12-oz) can pineapple pieces, drained
4 sprigs of borage

Put the ice cubes in a very large jug or punch bowl. Add all the remaining ingredients and stir well to blend. Serve at once.

Citrus ponets

Makes 2 litres/3¼ pints

METRIC/IMPERIAL
15 ice cubes
1·4 litres/2¼ pints white Rhine wine
150 ml/¼ pint vodka
150 ml/¼ pint soda water
juice of 6 medium oranges
juice of 2 large grapefruit
juice of 1 lemon
1 small pineapple, peeled and finely chopped
100 g/4 oz maraschino cherries

Place the ice cubes in a large punch bowl. Add all the remaining ingredients and mix well to blend. Serve at once.

INDEX

127